D1157935

PRAISE FOR *THE LIARS*

"Ida Linehan Young does well-researched well-paced melodrama well." — THE TELEGRAM

"There is no doubt that she is amongst the best of the best of Newfoundland's storytellers. . . . If you like good historical fiction stories told in a similar vein to Genevieve Graham's, then you'll enjoy this trilogy of turn-of-the-last-century novels from the prolific pen of Ida Linehan Young." — THE MIRAMICHI READER

"The storyline of mystery, intrigue, and plot twists that Linehan Young expertly crafts in *The Liars* is the result of true events that occurred in the late 1800s in Newfoundland. Her ability to formulate a fictitious story by intertwining research with plot details conceived in her mind is brilliant. *The Liars* is another compelling read for those who enjoy history, suspense, and wonderfully descriptive writing. The female characters are strong, simple, but complex individuals, who reinforce the theme that there is no greater warrior than a mother protecting her child. Kudos to Ida Linehan Young in creating a work of art that will leave you wanting more." — FIRESIDE COLLECTIONS

"Ida Linehan Young skilfully weaves this complicated tapestry from its first warp and woof on a loom in Labrador to its final hemstitch in North Harbour, St. Mary's Bay." — LOTP: LIFE ON THIS PLANET

PRAISE FOR *THE STOLEN ONES*

"*The Stolen Ones* is a modern-day story of love and loss, heartbreak and healing and provides proof that knowing one's roots can serve as a powerful antidote against adverse life experiences. The author does a superb job at crafting a tale that begins in modern-day Boston and then seamlessly moves back and forth from the present day to that of John's Pond, 1878. Readers will delight in the authenticity of the story and its main characters Darlene, Tiffany, and Aunt Ammie and will likewise be inspired by the tragedy and triumphs of the ancestral Nolan family. It is this mingling of past and present where the true story unfolds, new questions arise, and old mysteries are solved. Linehan Young's ability to weave facts into the fictional storyline is a testament to her love for the culture of her home province of Newfoundland and the rich art of storytelling that was passed down to her by her father and grandfather." — FIRESIDE COLLECTIONS

"Ida, you have me mesmerized. I tip my hat and applaud the author." — LOTP: LIFE ON THIS PLANET

IF I CRY
I'LL FILL
the OCEAN

BY IDA LINEHAN YOUNG

NON-FICTION

No Turning Back
If I Cry I'll Fill the Ocean

FICTION

Being Mary Ro
The Promise
The Liars
The Stolen Ones

IF I CRY
I'LL FILL
the OCEAN

THE CATHERINE LINEHAN STORY

Catherine Linehan

AS TOLD TO
IDA LINEHAN YOUNG

FLANKER PRESS LIMITED
ST. JOHN'S

Library and Archives Canada Cataloguing in Publication

Title: If I cry I'll fill the ocean : the Catherine Linehan story / as told to Ida Linehan Young.
Names: Linehan Young, Ida, 1964- author.
Identifiers: Canadiana (print) 20220161089 | Canadiana (ebook) 20220161135 | ISBN
    9781774570746 (softcover) | ISBN 9781774570753 (EPUB) | ISBN 9781774570760 (PDF)
Subjects: LCSH: Linehan, Catherine (Mother) | LCSH: Mothers—Newfoundland and Labra-
    dor—Biography. | LCSH: Fires—Casualties—Newfoundland and Labrador—North Har-
    bour (Saint Mary's Bay) | LCSH: Grief. | LCSH: Children—Death. | LCGFT: Biographies.
Classification: LCC FC2199.N59 Z49 2022 | DDC 363.3709718—dc23

PRINTED IN CANADA

MIX
Paper from
responsible sources
FSC® C016245

This paper has been certified to meet the environ-
mental and social standards of the Forest Stewardship
Council® (FSC®) and comes from responsibly managed forests, and verified recycled sources.

Cover Design by Graham Blair

FLANKER PRESS LTD.
PO BOX 2522, STATION C
ST. JOHN'S, NL
CANADA

TELEPHONE: (709) 739-4477   FAX: (709) 739-4420   TOLL-FREE: 1-866-739-4420
WWW.FLANKERPRESS.COM

9 8 7 6 5 4 3 2 1

Canada   Canada Council   Conseil des Arts   Newfoundland
         for the Arts   du Canada   Labrador

We acknowledge the [financial] support of the Government of Canada. *Nous reconnaissons l'appui [financier] du
gouvernement du Canada.* We acknowledge the support of the Canada Council for the Arts, which last year invested $153
million to bring the arts to Canadians throughout the country. *Nous remercions le Conseil des arts du Canada de son soutien.
L'an dernier, le Conseil a investi 153 millions de dollars pour mettre de l'art dans la vie des Canadiennes et des Canadiens
de tout le pays.* We acknowledge the financial support of the Government of Newfoundland and Labrador, Department of
Tourism, Culture and Recreation for our publishing activities.

Dedication

For the people in my riverbed and tributaries who taught me fortitude, resiliency, humour, and grace of spirit, heart, and soul.

First and foremost would be my mother, Catherine Linehan. She has been my strongest influencer, my biggest supporter, and the person who has loved me longest. Each of us could say that as truth.

Edward Linehan, my father. His outlook on life was as unfathomable and unshakable as his love of family. His honesty, his goodness, his trust in God, and his steadfast plod forward saturated us with the best of him.

Frank and Ida Power, my maternal grandparents. Their love and affection for each other and for their family helped define us all.

Francis, Richard, Sharon, Harold, and Barry Linehan, my brothers and sister. We only had a lend of them for a little while, but the comfort of their love is everlasting.

For those mentioned within these pages, and those who are known in our hearts, related by blood, by friendship, by kind deeds, or any other positive touch point or glancing blow, we thank you for being part of us. Especially for those rooted in the community of North Harbour, as always, your acts of kindness, charity, and bravery have not only been audible but laudable and appreciated.

Always for those who will keep my riverbed flowing: Sharon, Stacey, Shawna, Parker, and Sammy. I hope my own shaping and my love will be the solid foundation you need as you go forward. I hope my influence can help you face whatever the world throws at you with strength, resilience, and love.

CONTENTS

INTRODUCTION

A Daughter's Narrative

As I sit in quiet reflection on this day of great solemnity, my eyes can't help but explore the tall spruce, unremarkable among the others of its kind, yet standing out in its anonymity here in the graveyard. The embattled tree is tough, ragged, and strong. I imagine it has weathered years of calm and storms that only the tree itself knows. Its aging rugged presence does not reveal the harsh conditions of its past when it trembled and splintered in the hurricane, when it genuflected and fastened to the earth in the ice storm, or when it slumped beneath the heavy snows. It accepts its fate as a tree and what it was fashioned for.

My mother, like the tree, is inconspicuous by her nature. She, too, was dragged low by heavy burdens and managed to stand strong time and time again. However, after being devastated by one catastrophic event, she remains near-broken and unable to be righted. Her new form is not out of the ordinary to the beholder. The wound unseen and pinned to her soul for eternity is something only she bears. We can only speculate what she suffers and has suffered as rare glimpses of the unimaginable surface and etch her features with a longing to go back.

Although I have heard scraps of her history, I haven't heard it all at once. I interviewed her and prepared questions from the bits and pieces I knew. I hoped the conversation would fill in the rest and spur more questions. She sat across from me at the kitchen table, and we began.

She answered my questions openly and honestly, giving me new insight into her story. We laughed at some things, and we reflected on others. I leave the hardest questions until day three. The topic was sad. We didn't cry, though I must admit that I braced for the recollections, and I am certain she did, too.

As I absorb and put all the information together, I am in shock at how much one person can endure. It leads me to believe, if there is such a thing, she was being "prepared" for the heart-rending she got, one hardship at a time. Plundered by continual suffering, sadly, she is toughened to difficulty, loss, and adversity.

Since the events and aftermath of that awful day, I believe that my mother learned to "be" outwardly different, not because it's what she knowingly intends or is resigned to, but as the only way to maintain some semblance of sanity.

As life continues to ravage the conditions around her, she breathes in and breathes out, and she sleeps, and she wakes as she had learned before. She doesn't think to the other end of an ordeal, or to the end of life, really; she deals with it one breath at a time.

I've known for a long time that my mother can't allow "genuinity" of emotions—to laugh, or especially to cry without boundaries—because she might founder in a place where the "uns" come from—unimaginable, unbearable, unfathomable, unspeakable, and all the "un" words that may not even be thought up yet. These words encompass the weight of something enormous and difficult and rare. She adjusts to, but cannot escape, the unending lament that she lives with every day—it stains her heart and will remain there until she dies.

You see her pain has no cure. It cannot be banished nor erased. There are no words to ease sorrow; it is a burden carried alone, and each one's load is different, and the load is not constantly the same nor distributed evenly.

Building immunity to emotion has been her defence. This is sometimes viewed by others as strength. And in many ways, it is, the old-fashioned, soul-changing strength that stood the test of time for centuries. Now with the modern and "patternized" stages of grief, there comes certain expectations that she should have or will have passed each stage and have "gotten over it."

Those who know her well say she is a woman of great faith. While that is true, there is also anticipation that comes with belief. It is an unknown that allows hope to reign and possibilities to foster and life to go on. Faith allows her to live in hope rather than to go toward death in despair. Paired with her strength, she can continue to hold fast to a facade that is untelling of the hardship and the struggle of her life. Like the tree, she wears the present, not the past, and what her heart has borne cannot be seen.

In order to maintain this armour, simply put, my mother couldn't and doesn't allow herself to grieve. At first it was because there were so many immediacies to attend to and roles to play. Then later, a busyness was found to occupy the emptiness. The wordless sorrow that she holds inside all but strangles her, yet it swaddles memories of before. She can't let go.

She lives a layered life in many ways. The top layer is where she smiles, jokes around, plays cards, prays, and gets about daily life. The underneath coddles the complex yet simpler cares of yesteryear. Never the twain shall meet, because as she says, if she thinks about it, she'll cry, and if she cries, she'll fill the ocean.

As time continues, as only time can do so well, she has learned to live unnaturally in a before and after compartmentalized life. Unable to go back, and with life dragging her forward, she has found a way of being that's tolerable and instinctive. Struggle is ingrained in her reality. Living is good enough. It's not something that she can either accept or reject—as with the spruce, it's just the way of it.

The covered scar is unseen by those who don't know what is hidden, as is the strain the soul endures. She is accustomed to holding at bay a bitter emptiness of the events that slashed the jagged chasm, dividing the two spaces. It is embroidered in the depths of her soul. But, with forewarning and endless clenching to maintain sanity, she mostly manages to keep the wound tethered so that it doesn't destroy her. There are times a name, or a date, or a memory grab onto her without mercy, and grief percolates and seeps out. But she breathes in, she breathes out, she sleeps, she wakes, and she continues to "be" the way she has learned. Her penance for loving remains within the boundaries she has set in the before and after times.

For those who consider the old saying "time heals everything" to be a truth, they have been fortunate enough not to have borne one of those "everythings" that exist to be unmended. A swath of sorrow and anguish may be concealed, but the underlying wounds can be scraped and exposed as fresh and as raw as the day they were struck. What could be contrived as healing is, in fact, masking—the face untelling of the hurt that lies beneath.

Concealing within the bounds of faith and strength is what saves her from an outward-facing and torturous sorrow. Time makes it possible to become more accustomed to maintaining the ruse. There is absolutely no judgment in that. It is what is necessary. It is the way of it; the only way of it for her. When faced with it, I don't know that anyone could or would do differently. I have the deepest admiration and love for my mother. I strive to have her faith, her strength, and her hope.

I am blessed and honoured to be able to put her extraordinary life's story to paper. She is not Queen Elizabeth, nor Joan of Arc, nor Amelia Earhart, nor will she be recorded in the annals of history. She is Catherine (Power) Linehan from North Harbour, St. Mary's Bay, and an inspiration to many whom she's encountered over the years.

Everything written here is as she described it to me. My only hope is that I can find the words her story deserves.

To understand the present, you must also look to the past. Heredity, both the DNA and the characteristics you display, shapes the riverbeds through which your waters run. In order to understand my mother and her outlook on life, first you must be introduced to her parents and their story as well as where she came from.

North Harbour, a tiny inlet cleaved into the northern part of St. Mary's Bay, has been the base of the storied life of our family for five generations and more than a hundred years' worth of living and dying. The harbour is mainly settled on the north today, with few inhabitants on the tiny finger of land on the south side known locally as "the other side." When the community flourished during the height of the fishery, there were 200–300 residents on both sides of the harbour. Until the road came through from Colinet in the 1960s to "the other side," the only way in or out was by boat or on foot. It wasn't until the late 1970s that the road connected Branch to the south and North Harbour became part of a driving loop and the community lost its isolation. The remoteness plays a part in how the tale unfolds.

My maternal grandparents met at a dance on the south side of North Harbour or, as we would say, on the other side.

As the story goes, my grandfather, Frank Power, from Bristol's Hope in Conception Bay, was shipwrecked in St. Mary's Bay. The stranded men from the boat were picked up by local fishermen and transported to various home ports. My grandfather and a couple of the crew were brought to the other side by the Whalens, who were fishing near the wreck at the time.

To welcome the strangers, a dance was planned at Whalen's. Without a community hall, dances were commonplace in kitchens, leading to the modern-day "kitchen party." My grandfather, an outstanding accordion player, volunteered to play in gratitude for the civility of the hosts.

My grandmother, Ida Power, got wind of the dance, in those days "the time," and set to planning how she would cross the harbour to partake. She loved to dance and socialize. Every opportunity in a small harbour where such goings-on were a rarity, especially during the fishing season, was a coveted affair.

Ida was the youngest in the family of thirteen children. Her father died when she was eleven, and her mother before Nanny turned eighteen. She lived with two older brothers, Ben and Bill, as well as an older sister, Mary. Mary, who was five years older than my grandmother, would have been considered in those times as "simple," but today she would be determined to have special needs. Although Ben married later in life, Bill remained a bachelor and became the provider for both Nanny and Mary after their parents' deaths. Sadly, Mary died at the age of thirty-three, almost ten years after her mother.

At Whalen's that evening, the wood stove was put out by the door, and my grandfather played square sets and step dances in the kitchen. When my grandmother arrived and my grandfather first laid eyes on her, he told his "bandmate," one of the crewmen who'd been shipwrecked with him, "I'm going to marry that girl," and he meant it. He managed to introduce himself, not caring if she was "spoken for" or not, and, in fact, she wasn't. For the entire night, until the sun crept upon them the next morning, my grandmother danced with whomever didn't have a partner at any given time, and my grandfather played.

Within a couple of weeks, the shipwrecked crew were picked up by the new vessel of the enterprise, and the men went on about their skipper's business at sea. My grandfather saw as much of Nanny as he could, and before leaving, he expressed his intentions of a relationship to my grandmother. That was how their courtship began.

Grandfather was a sailor and a sealer from the time he was old enough to get a berth. When he made it to home port in Harbour Grace, and when time allowed it, he walked the railway bed to Whitbourne and then out a dirt track to North Harbour to see her—a distance of about sixty miles or almost 100 kilometres. That often took him an entire day to make the journey from start to finish. Sometimes, if the weather was bad or it got too dark on him, he stayed in a stable somewhere along the route and continued on to see her the next morning. He might only get to spend a day with her, but it didn't matter. They were meant to be together and their relationship fated.

They married in 1924 at St. Patrick's Church in St. John's and moved to the Goulds, to the house of her father-in-law. Grandfather was away on the boats a great deal of time, and Nanny looked after his father, who by this time had become frail. She had a son, Frank, and was pregnant on her second boy, Richard (Dick), when the old man became bedridden. My grandfather rigged up a sling to the ceiling so it would be easier for her to move him. The old man was afraid she was going to hurt herself in her care of him.

When my maternal great-grandfather died, Nanny refused to stay by herself and returned to North Harbour every time my grandfather was at sea. Eventually, they moved to the other side of North Harbour and lived in an old and ramshackle two-storey house. Every night that Grandfather was away, Nanny took the children and stayed with her sister Annie, who lived about a half a mile from her. She didn't want to be alone in the dark. She didn't mind during the days, but she hated the nights. Nanny fretted until Grandfather came home to her. She was also petrified of wind and walked the floors, no matter where she stayed, if it was a windy night.

After less than a year of life on the other side, they decided to move to my grandmother's parents' house on the north side of the harbour. It was vacant, but it was also old and drafty, and after a few years, it became unfit to live in. Her brother Bill, who by this time was living alone, developed a condition called dropsy and became quite feeble. He needed special food and help with feeding. My grandmother took on that duty, and they moved to his house, which had better living conditions for her growing family.

By this time, my mother, Catherine, and her older sister, Mary (May), were born. Nanny was glad for the company of her brother and, for the first time, didn't need to find a place to stay at night when Grandfather was gone.

But Grandfather knew how lonely she got when he was away and how much she wanted him to stay home, so he took on a berth with a local fisherman and was home mostly every night. My mother said he made some kind of living at it and had given up on his passion so he could be with my grandmother. It wasn't a sacrifice; it was just what he did out of love for her.

My mother, being the youngest girl, grew up having a close bond with Nanny. She watched, as well as helped, her care for her uncle Bill for years before he died. Many things she did in her youth were influenced by the knowledge that Nanny didn't like to be alone and that she was a caregiver at heart.

Even when we were growing up, every night my mother walked the mile or so to my grandparents' house and spent a few hours with them before they went to bed. It was a ritual that we took for granted for many years. After my grandfather died, Mom took Nanny in to live with her and my father. There, my grandmother fretted for over two years as she waited to "go with her old man."

My grandparents had an incredibly unique and loving relationship that was often remarked on by many. Even when they received their old-age security pensions, they walked to the general store, arm in arm, to get their month's groceries. People said they were "right united," but today we would say they deeply loved one another until the end of their days. We often romanticized their connection. However, a loving relationship didn't necessarily equate to an easy life. They saw poverty and hard times, but they saw it together.

Their rapport as a couple, and the bond that my mother had with her mother, helped shape our whole family, and will hopefully trickle down for generations. We had a backdrop of love, kindness, and caring for others. It fashioned my mother's story in many ways. And that story will unfold in her own voice in the following chapters.

PROLOGUE

The Dream

"Mommy, I can't see," Barry says, his voice hoarse as he cries out to me. He coughs. I squeeze my eyes tight and shake my head.

"Where are you?" I ask as fear surfaces like a shark ready to devour me.

"I can't see. I can't see." His frantic voice is somewhere in the smoky distance.

"I'm coming. I'm coming. I'll save you," I repeat as I grope my way along the hall.

"Mommy," he cries. "I'm over here."

His voice is near in the blackness. I reach out my hand and grab him by the arm. "Come on, we must hurry." My breaths are matching my fast pace as smoke fills in around me.

I pull him along behind me as I quickly retrace my way across the hall, then down the stairs and out into the yard.

"You're safe now, my little boy."

I look down, but Barry isn't there. I must go back. Where is he? How did I lose him?

I'm back in my room.

Barry's voice is there again, above the noise. "Mommy, I can't see." He sounds frantic. My heart pounds in desperation. I scramble across the hall once again, retracing what I'd done a million times. The smoke is thicker now. I push along the wall and feel for the door opening, following Barry's voice.

"I'm coming. I'll save you."

The recycling scene is not lost on me, but I still have to act as I reach him again. I grab his hand and pull him along behind me. In the yard, I warn him to stay there while I go in for Harold. I race up the stairs and across the hall, my breathing laboured from the smoke and the exertion. I call to Harold, but there's no answer. Francis must have him. Francis would have known how to get out. He's older, of course he knows. I rush back down the stairs calling their names.

"Francis."

"Richard."

"Sharon."

"Harold."

"Barry."

I swim my way through the smoke, frustrated that nobody is answering, and my hands are pushing the toxic air away as I make my way toward the light from the door. I'm alone in the meadow. Barry is gone. I hear him cry out from inside the house. "Mommy, I can't see."

How did he get back there? I bolt for the door one more time and make my way toward his voice. I grab him and pull him to the door in the room. "Feel your way along the wall. I need to find Harold. The way out is that way." I push him toward where my voice has directed him to the top of the stairs. My heart pounds as I grab the bedclothes and pat them for signs of a leg or an arm or a head. My knees are pinched by the bedsprings as I throw myself across the mattress. Nobody is there. The smoke is thicker now. There's a roaring in my ears. I drag myself off the bed and across the hall. I don't meet Barry. I don't hear him now. He must be outside. I burst into the sunlight, my breaths coming in gasps.

"Barry, where are you?"

"Mommy, I can't see."

I open my eyes and look around. I'm no longer in the meadow. The light is sharp and burns. Where am I? The white of the ceiling comes into focus as I grab the bedrail.

"Barry," I say softly. Barry is gone.

I'm awake, my dream has ended.

"Barry is gone," I repeat with resignation and sadness.

My life is ending.

I think about that now.

Catherine Linehan
Age 88, December 1, 2021

Part I

The Before Compartment

1

Carefree Childhood Times

I loved to be outside. You could say I had a bit of a tomboy streak. I liked to help my father cut and haul wood, or helped in the garden when there was planting, but I just didn't like the housework part that came with staying in. My father didn't mind nor discourage it.

One of my friends had no choice in the matter of being inside. Her circumstances of being motherless, her father feeding a big family, and he and her older brothers fishing, meant she and her sisters had to go home after school to do chores. She didn't complain, though. I was happy that Mom didn't make me come home and our family was a lot smaller.

As a matter of fact, Mom didn't make me go to school the first year I was eligible, either. I was supposed to go to grade one a few weeks before I turned five. I went for a few minutes in the morning, didn't like it, was lonesome, and wouldn't stay. Mom allowed me to wait until the next year.

Outside work didn't seem like chores. My father had an old

handcat, as we called it. I helped him tow that sled to the woods. He'd push while I took the lead and pulled it over the rugged and browcey path to the top of the ridge behind the house. At the crest, the going got easier. I'd pile it with wood as he pared it out with the axe. We'd have maybe ten or fifteen small and twisted sticks on the load. We had to criss-cross the hill so as not to lose the sled on the way out. Sometimes I imagined the handcat taking off and ramming into the back of the house.

The neighbours often joked that my father had every letter of the alphabet in the woodpile except for the letter "I." He didn't care; he said it would all burn.

I don't remember my father as being overly affectionate as such, but he invited and often expected me to join him doing his chores. Mom didn't make me stay in and bake bread or wash clothes, though I often helped her with painting, or looming and dying wool.

I can still see the hanks of yarn draped over the fence to dry. There was a lot of work went into that. One of my uncles would give us a flour sack full of wool after the sheep were sheared in the spring. First we had to wash it and pick out debris like sticks and twigs that would have been tangled up over the winter as the sheep took to the woods. Then she'd wash it in a big aluminum tub, afterwards laying it out on the grass to dry. One of my tasks was to turn it over so the sun could dry it faster. Then Mom carded the wool. It was mostly white, but if we were lucky enough to have wool from a black sheep, she'd be able to make grey yarn.

Mom didn't have a spindle, but Uncle Bill made her the wheel part after she got married. When she was ready to spin the yarn, she'd borrow a spindle from one of her brothers or sisters and attach it to the wheel. After the wool was carded, I'd help her spin it.

Once she had enough for a hank of yarn, she'd wash that again and hang it on the fence to dry. Sometimes she bought red dye and made pink wool to knit socks and mittens for myself and May.

She taught me to knit one winter when I was a young girl, maybe nine or ten years old. She showed me how to turn the double-knit heel and close out the toe, and I still do it the same way. I helped her make socks and mitts for the whole family.

But, in the end, I would rather dig a ditch than knit or bake bread. Mom understood this in me and didn't discourage it. Since there were only six of us, including Mom and Dad, I was more fortunate than my friends, who had to help when most of their families had ten-plus children.

So, I got the love of the outdoors from my father, though I was fun-loving, which was more of a trait from my mother. I lived carefree days as a young girl but learned enough from my mother to get by when I had to.

Some of my fondest memories are from when all hands that were allowed played baseball in the meadow not far from the school. There were as many, if not more, girls than boys. In those days, there were no gloves. If you had possession of the old hard ball and you saw somebody running from one base to the next, you'd pelt the ball at them with whatever strength you had. It didn't matter where you hit them, in the legs, on the head, in the back. If you hit them while they were off the base, they were out. It used to be a lot of fun. But, I have to say, the ball did hurt. I was a good shot, though, and rarely missed a target.

Some days, before the school bell rang, me and my friends threw fist-sized rocks up in a great big spruce tree. We had to run in under the tree and throw the rock up over our heads and then run out. I did that one day, and somebody else's rock was still up there and shook loose. It came down on top of my head. It skinned me right out, took the hair and everything off that spot. The girls laughed at me. Mom fixed me up when I went home, but she didn't say a word about the foolishness we were up to.

My friend Deborah Bonia lived way up on the other end of the harbour. She was a year younger than me, but we met in the old schoolhouse and became friends. It took a long time to walk there, especially as a kid of nine or ten, but one summer I wouldn't want to be anywhere else.

Deborah was an only child, so her mother, Mrs. Marie, encouraged me to go there, and also with her encouragement, we decided to have a concert. Every fine day for a few weeks that year I'd go up the harbour. We'd spend time in the stable and practise our singing.

The horse pound was a bit higher than the floor, so that became our stage. Mrs. Marie set up drapes on a wooden pole. She rigged a string onto them to make the curtains open and close. Both Deborah and I practised our songs daily. When Mrs. Marie said we were more than ready, she invited my mother and a couple of others to come to the concert.

We were so proud that day. We sang our hearts out. The curtains opened, we'd sing and then bow after each song, before the curtains closed again. The crowd of three or four clapped heartily, and I believed it was the best summer of our young lives.

As teenagers, we'd walk up and down our side of the harbour and sing songs at the top of our lungs until we had to go in for the night. You could hear us plain enough, even over on the other side across the water. Patricia and Margaret, the Walsh sisters, were part of the group. They were great singers, and though Mary Power wasn't that good, I was all right at it. In the end, it didn't matter, we all sang anyway, as if the harbour was our stage. Enjoyment came with no cost.

Late in my teenaged years, I loved to go to dances. I never wanted to be tied down with a boyfriend, because then I might not be allowed to go. My sister, May, didn't go to dances, because her boyfriend wouldn't go. He was afraid he'd lose her. I wasn't going to be in that predicament when there was fun to be had. I often told May that, but she was content and didn't listen to me. Boys and girls hung out by an old mill, a scattered fellow would walk me home, but that was it. I wanted nothing to do with anything that I thought would confine me.

Lots of times, boats from what we called the "Wester," or Fortune and Placentia Bays, sheltered from the winds up in what we called the pond. There'd be little wind behind the two points that gave access to the pond from the harbour, and often eight to ten boats would be there all at once. Boats meant dances in a house on one side or the other.

If I heard of a dance and could get there, I'd be gone. One time, me, John Power, Seb Walsh, and Mary Power learned of a dance in a house on the other side. We had no way across, so we decided to borrow (without asking) Uncle Ben's dory.

The dory was pulled up by his house, so we crept in and picked it up and brought it down to the beach. We were in such a hurry, afraid we'd get caught, that we shoved off the dory and Mary tried to jump in and fell on her back in the pound. We were laughing that hard, we thought Uncle Ben would hear us. Somehow, that made the excitement even greater. We ducked down and tittered until the danger of being seen had passed.

We made it to the other side and danced all night. When the dance was over and we had to leave, the wind had come up. Seb and John wouldn't row across the harbour, but they would try and get to the sandy point on our side. That was only a small distance. When we crossed, we pulled the dory as far up under the trees as we could and walked the few miles home.

The next day, Uncle Ben looked everywhere for the dory, and when he found it up on the point, he swore that he'd do away with whoever put her there if he could find out who it was. We wouldn't tell him for fear we'd get in trouble. I'm sure my mother knew but didn't say anything.

Despite my love of gallivanting, there were times, though, if there was a dance and I knew Mom was home by herself after Uncle Bill died, I'd leave early and go home with her, because I knew she was afraid. She wouldn't want me to do that, but I could tell by the way her shoulders relaxed and her eyes lit up she was glad I did.

Overall, I can't say I had a bad childhood. It was fun and carefree. We didn't have very much, but nobody did. I'm sure my parents struggled to make ends meet, but I didn't see it. We didn't go hungry, we weren't cold, and we were loved.

2

And Then There Were Three

I do remember an awful time in my childhood when I was fourteen. It was summer. I was in bed, and it wasn't far past daylight when a terrible scream made me sit bolt upright in the bed. It was my mother. I was disoriented at first, but I jumped out from under the quilt and caught sight of Mom and my father through the window. She was leaning across the gate, my father had a hold on her, and she was wailing.

I tore from the bed, down the stairs, and ran out the lane in my bare feet with my nightdress blowing in the breeze.

"Poor Frank. Poor Frank," she repeated between sobs as she gasped for breath and bent over the gate.

I was confused by the words I was hearing from my father as he discussed something with my uncle.

Recover. Drowned.

Body.

I wasn't grasping what was happening in my haste to get to and comfort my mother.

My father helped keep Mom from collapsing on the rocks as her legs gave out and she continued to screech. "Poor Frank. Poor Frank." Her voice rang out in the clear morning and echoed off the land across the harbour.

I moved around to my mother's side and took her weight to hold her upright. I understood they were talking about my oldest brother, but it took me a while to realize what they were saying.

Frank was dead. He had drowned.

Frank had left the evening before with two other fellows to go to Cape Dog to catch salmon. It normally took several hours to walk. The young men had planned to set a net on the river and wait out there until morning for the catch. This wasn't legal at the time but was a practice that many participated in, especially with poor times and bare pantries.

From what I learned later that day, the two others had waited on one side of the river and had sent Frank across to the other side in an old soggy dory to set the net. The river was wide and deep, and the little boat swamped. Frank ended up in the water, and none of them could swim. Because it was dark, it was a few hours before the two could get back to North Harbour to tell what had happened.

Several men left and walked to Cape Dog to retrieve my brother's body. Dick was away working in Stephenville, on the other side of the island, at the time. Later that day, my father sent a telegram to notify Dick of what had happened.

Braced on one side of her and my father on the other, with arms linked in through Mom's, we all but carried her into the house. There we waited. My thoughts were scrambled as I tried in vain to comfort her. I made her tea, but she wouldn't drink;

I got her toast, but she wouldn't eat. She cried and cried, and I had no way to help her. I didn't know what to do; my insides were in turmoil. I cried for my mother, or maybe I cried because she cried. People came and gathered and watched the hand on the timepiece with us.

Around mid-morning, Frank was carried in. My mother was a renewed frantic. She screamed and cried out his name, "Poor Frank," over and over as she clawed at the air to get to him. My father held her back.

Upon hearing of the tragedy, in the early morning hours, my cousin Feb (Fabian Linehan) crossed the harbour to the mill and purchased lumber to make a casket. He went back to his shed and began his grim task. Before Frank was brought home, Feb was rowing across the harbour with a box across the front of the dory. He landed in the beach below our meadow, and a few men from the community carried it up over the steep bank and as far as the house. It remained poised and ready for its purpose, there in the yard, leaking turpentine tears in the hot sun. Its duty to be ready for Frank, when Frank was ready for it.

My brother was washed and prepared for the wake by two women who were no strangers to the task. Behind closed doors, my brother was made ready to be laid out. As was tradition, he needed to be dressed in the finest that was ill-afforded. All we had home was my father's dark grey suit in the trunk. He had purchased it many years before when he was sailing on the boats in one foreign land or another. I believe he was keeping it for his own burial. Though it was too big for my brother, it was all that we had. Frank would have the best.

The scant furnishings were shifted around my mother to make room for the goings-on of the next few days. She sat in the chair at the end of the table while the mourners circled her. She was inconsolable. I tried to act like her because I didn't know what else to do. She cried for the three days he was laid out in the front room, and I did the same when people were around.

The first time I was alone with my brother, I touched Frank's face, and he felt warm to me. I was confused and thought he was sleeping. I wiped tears from his eyes and nudged him to wake up. There was a little fly circling his face, and his nose bubbled. I heard soft moaning sounds coming from him. But when anyone came in the room, I sat dutifully on the chair, I cried, and I didn't say a word.

I watched for opportunities to be alone with him. I tried repeatedly to get him to wake up before it was too late. He didn't respond. Nobody else seemed to think it was odd, though every bit of me was screaming for somebody to notice. It couldn't be me to speak up, as I was too young to know such things. Others wiped his tears and dismissed the sounds. To my young eyes, he wept as much as my mother.

I had dreams after he was buried. I imagined him tearing at the inside of the spruce box to get free. The image stayed with me a long time. I regretted that I didn't or couldn't speak up; I regretted my youthfulness; and I regretted that it was not my place.

Frank was twenty years old. I watched my mother grieve for her son. It was eternal. She changed after that. Her face was sad, her eyes weepy, especially when she was alone. Any time she spoke his name, it was forever "poor Frank" this or "poor Frank" that.

Dick arrived almost a week later. He stayed for a little while and then went back to work on the other side of the island. As the youngest, I became more protective of my mother. I felt guilty that Frank wasn't alive and believed that it was because of me not saying anything that he was gone from the house. I often thought of him trying to get out and listened for him for years when passing the graveyard. I didn't know how long he could last, nor did I understand what death from drowning did to a body.

That was my first experience with death. My uncle Bill, whom we lived with, had died five years before, but I was too young to remember much about it.

I took on the brunt of my mother's hurt because I didn't speak up. May left shortly after Frank's passing and went to work in Goose Bay, in Labrador. I stayed home with Mom. I remained in school until after I was sixteen, because the government paid $5 a month in a bursary at the time. Mom and Dad needed the money.

I was close to my mother and wanted nothing more than to ease her sorrow.

3

Stumbling into Love

With my father fishing locally and no longer away for long periods of time, it was easier to go to dances, and boy, didn't I ever love that. I got boat rides to the Island (Colinet Island), the Beach (Admiral's Beach), Mount Carmel, and Colinet. A bunch of us would leave before supper, either on foot or by boat, and get back sometime early in the daylight hours. During the summer when the parish garden parties were on the go, that's when the dances were plentiful, and I went to every one that I could.

The garden party dance was coming up in Mount Carmel, and my cousin Paul was going. He had room for me in the boat, and I was ecstatic to have a way over. We got ready just after our lunch, and Paul landed us across to the other side in his skiff. We walked to John's Pond, a couple of miles over the hill. From there we went in Mr. Jim Dalton's boat, along with a crowd from John's Pond, as far as the Tickles. Once we landed in the Tickles, we walked to Harricott, another few miles, and got aboard the back of an old stake-bodied truck belonging to Mr. Dinn Gregory.

He took us over a bumpy and dusty dirt road to the parish hall in Mount Carmel. That was where I met Eddy Linehan. He was born in John's Pond, but he lived in Holyrood for many years and had come to the dance with friends.

We danced together all night. I was smitten. He returned as far as John's Pond to stay the night, and I went back home with Paul to North Harbour. My cousin Bridie was married to Dave Dalton from John's Pond. Eddy asked her about me. He realized he knew my brother Dick. Within a few days he came over to our house to see my parents, as well as Dick and, by proximity, me.

Eddy worked on the other side of the island in the "lumber woods" in Badger. Dick was working there now as well. Despite being sixteen years my senior, Eddy came to see me and my parents the few times he was back on the east coast.

Just before I turned eighteen, I got a job at Bennett's, a large nursing home in Holyrood. My mother gave me the few dollars that she had, and I caught a taxi in Colinet, with the intent to stay at Bennett's while I was working and go home every couple of weeks or, at least, once a month.

When I arrived, Mrs. Bennett put piles and piles of white sheets in front of me and told me I had to iron them all, fold them, and put them away. I spent the entire day doing this chore, as the sheets and laundry didn't lessen no matter how many I finished. I knew it would be the same for the next day and the next.

Eddy, who lived not far from there, came to see me later in the day. I told him I wasn't staying, and that was that. He arranged for a taxi to pick me up at the end of the workday. I took the few dollars I had earned and went to stay with my aunt Annie in St. John's. I had big notions of finding my way in the world.

My first job in St. John's was at a place called "The Palace" behind the Basilica of St. John the Baptist. It was the house where the priests and the bishop stayed. My friends from North Harbour were working there, Patricia and Margaret Walsh. I wasn't cut out for serving tea and meals, so I left there and went to a cleaning job at the home of a well-to-do St. John's family. That didn't work out too well after the head maid told me that my floor waxing skills weren't good, especially after she walked over the freshly waxed area without giving it a chance to dry. I told her that if she wanted it any better, she'd have to do it herself. I didn't last at that job very long with that attitude. But I couldn't see myself doing it forever, either.

Next, I got a job as a maid at the Cochrane Hotel. That's where I met a girl named Bride Nash from Branch. She'd been there for a few years and took me under her wing and looked out for me. She taught me how to smoke. I wasn't keen on it first, but she kept offering and showing me how to inhale without coughing. I got hooked. It would be twenty-six years later, November 4, 1977, when my cousin Paul died from throat cancer, that I'd lift the damper and throw my cigarettes in the stove. Though I was smoking two packs a day by then, I didn't bother them again.

I quit at the hotel and went to the Waterford Hospital, where I got a job as a nursing assistant. The pay was better. I stayed in the dormitory with some of the other workers for almost a year. I wasn't as content as I thought I'd be, although I did enjoy the work. I don't know if I was scared at night or if I was just lonesome for home. There were awful noises, especially after dark. Sometimes it was the girls trying to frighten each other, and sometimes it was patients.

I began dating Eddy around that time. We'd see each other any chance we could, which really was not too often, with both our schedules.

After a year working at the Waterford making $75 a month, I was asked if I wanted to train as a nurse. I was excited for this opportunity and was considering that I'd possibly be a nurse all my life. There was a course I had to take, and it was costly. I didn't really have the money and was second-guessing myself about staying there, so I thought hard about the commitment.

Then, there was a lady admitted there that I knew from the other side of the bay. She had to undergo "shock treatment." Seeing what happened to her really affected me and was the catalyst for a complete change in how I'd spend the rest of my life.

Without the nursing assistant course, I had to leave the job I was in. So, when another came up at the old General Hospital in the kitchen, I was eager to take it. This one paid an extra dollar per month.

During that year I bought a coat and clothes for myself. I'd buy what I wanted at Wilansky's on Water Street and pay $5 per month on them until they were paid off.

But in the kitchen, I worked long hours. Though I stayed at the dormitory on the premises, I visited Aunt Annie a few times a month. I grew pale and thin and ate very little while working at the old General. Aunt Annie was worried about me and told me one day to go home, spend some time with my parents, and see if I'd feel better. It had been a while since I was able to make the trip due to shift work at the hospital, so I went, with her encouragement. If I didn't, I'm sure Aunt Annie would have sent after my mother to come for me and take me home.

Getting back home was like a tonic for me. I ate, I slept, and felt a general sense of well-being. It had been what I needed. Thoughts of going back to work grew heavy on me.

Then Eddy asked me to marry him, and it was settled. I wouldn't worry about being a nurse or a kitchen worker; I would move to John's Pond and be his wife. Eddy had built a house there where his parents' place had been. I told myself that it was as good a life as I would want.

The wedding wasn't a grand affair, by no means. I wasn't going to wear a white dress. It was the middle of February and too cold for that. Eddy bought me a light blue lined suit, long skirt, and jacket for my wedding outfit. I dressed at my parents' place, and Paul took me and my father across the harbour in a boat. Paul had an old truck there, because the road had come down to the other side from Colinet by then.

He drove us to Mount Carmel, where Eddy and I were wed. We returned to North Harbour, where Mom had the wedding feast prepared. There were several sittings, because the house was small. We had roast pork and vegetables from the garden. Eddy bought a wedding cake at Didham's in Colinet so my mother wouldn't have that chore nor have to spend money she didn't have.

After the meal, there was a time in the hall, where we danced all night. In the early hours of the morning, Paul landed us across to the other side, and we walked to John's Pond, in the bitter cold, to start life as man and wife. That was in February 1953; I would be twenty years old that September.

4

And Then There Were Twelve

In John's Pond, Eddy started a garden as soon as the snow was gone. We planted potatoes, turnip, and cabbage. He had lots of wood home for a couple of winters, but he wanted to be prepared. That first winter, I joined him and helped to cut and pare the trees, then carried the sticks to load on the horse and sled. At home the effort continued with unloading and piling.

He went back to Badger for work, and I didn't want to stay by myself. I had Mom come over and stay with me sometimes, and other times I went to North Harbour with her. Eddy would get home before Christmas for a few months, and we'd live in the house. He worked on the upstairs every opportunity he could spare, and we slept on the main floor until he could finish it.

In the summer of 1954, Mary was born. I stayed in Placentia for a few weeks prior with some cousins living there. Shortly after bringing her home, I sensed there was something wrong. I had no experience with babies, but things just didn't feel right. Mary couldn't keep down her milk. She was thin and white and listless. Mom came and stayed with me for a while when Eddy went back to work. She knew there was something wrong as well. In the end I had to take Mary to the cottage hospital in Placentia. After many trips, she'd be treated for infections, but nothing really changed.

When Mary was about nine months old, she was so thin, I'd take her up and she didn't have strength enough to cry. She couldn't lift her head. This trip to the hospital in Placentia, they admitted her. There was a Mrs. Linehan from Colinet in the hospital at the same time. She'd send word home to me about how Mary was doing. It was hard being home with the baby somewhere else, especially when I didn't know if she'd live or die. Mrs. Linehan's contact was welcome news.

This stay in hospital they figured out Mary was allergic to milk. We ended up having to buy Farmers white yellow label for her. That was hard to come by and expensive, but it didn't matter. It was what she needed.

Mary perked up for a month or so before her sickness returned. We brought her to Placentia again. She had no sooner been admitted when she got the chicken pox. The hospital sent word that she had to be moved to the Fever Hospital in St. John's. Once the chicken pox cleared, they brought her back.

She was in the hospital in Placentia on her second birthday in July. They called and told me they had an appointment for her with a specialist at the Janeway and that I could take her home until the appointment. I went for her the next day. The note said the appointment was scheduled in two weeks' time.

When I was leaving the hospital, Dr. Daly, who was an intern there at the time, followed me out to the door.

"Mrs. Linehan," he said in a low voice as he flicked his eyes back toward the corridor. I stared at him while holding Mary tightly in my arms. I grunted an acknowledgement that I was listening, too overcome with worry to do anything else at the time.

"Mrs. Linehan, if this were my child, I wouldn't wait for two weeks. I would go on to St. John's with her."

I squinted at him, my face curled in worry and my eyes full of questions.

"Please take her in today. Don't bring her home," he said. "I don't think she'll make it to the appointment."

My eyes widened in shock and fear when he said that, and he nodded gravely.

I called the taxi and went to St. John's with her, ending up at Aunt Annie's again. I'll be forever grateful that she continually had her doors open to me no matter how many were there.

Luckily, there was a fellow staying there from the Southern Shore. He was boarding with her at the time. Mary was whining and crying, and I was trying to keep her quiet, walking the floor, so as not to disturb the stranger.

This fellow looked at Mary and knew she was very sick. He mentioned his doctor, a Dr. Joy who had a clinic only a few minutes' walk from there. He offered to go with me. He walked ahead of us, leading the way, as we scurried up the hill toward the clinic.

I was pacing the small waiting room with Mary when Dr. Joy came out to get a file from the secretary behind the desk. The man who took me there tried to get the secretary to take us in. Dr. Joy listened for a second, then heard Mary and looked out at us. He dropped what he had in his hand and came immediately around the desk. He took Mary from me. She was limp and folded in over his hands. She didn't protest going to a stranger. He motioned for me to follow him to a room in the back.

"This child has no blood," he said. "Her colour alone . . . she's so white." He drew his fingers along her neck. "The veins are sticking out." He called for an ambulance. Mary was in the Janeway Hospital for a few months after that.

I'd go to St. John's when I could, but with no money, that wasn't often. Eddy had to come down from Badger a few times that summer and sent money when he could. When Mary got home, Eddy bought special small tins of food for her, little vegetables and fruits. Aunt Rose grew carrots and brought them every day to boil for Mary. She did perk up for a while.

Eddy sent telegrams asking about her, asking if he needed to come home. By the time he was finished in the lumber woods that fall, Mary was doing better.

Young Eddy was born in January 1957 during the biggest sleet storm in years. I stayed to Aunt Annie's while Mom took care of Mary. When it was time to go to the hospital, I had to call the police to come get me. Nellie, Aunt Annie's daughter, accompanied me, and she wasn't too pleased when the police car brought her home and all the neighbours saw her.

By the time I could take (little) Eddy home, Mom had let me know that Mary wasn't well. She was sick and became thin and poorly over the coming months. She spent a lot of time in the Janeway while the doctors tried to figure out what was going on.

I sent messages every day that somebody was going to Colinet to find out how she was doing. One day, Paul came in and told me that the hospital wanted me to go out the next day. I brought the baby over to my mother and got the taxi in the morning.

The doctors told me they thought Mary had leukemia. I'd never heard of it, and when they said cancer, I thought she was finished. I had to sign for her to have a bone marrow test. I'll never forget the howls from Mary during the exam.

Fortunately, after a bone marrow test, they ruled out leukemia. But the doctors still couldn't figure out what was wrong. I went back home that evening without her once more. Several days later they diagnosed her with celiac disease. Mary was allergic to bread.

Bread in the house and at mealtime was as common as grass in the meadow. Toast and tea were breakfast staples every day. That had to change for Mary. We ordered special flour and more specialized tins of food from St. John's. Mary was doing a whole lot better, and when all was said and done, that was the main thing.

Mom and Dad were in St. John's for appointments one day and bought flour and other supplies for us. These things were expensive, and my parents didn't have much, but Mom wanted to make sure Mary had what she needed. She came to the house the next day, and I went to work mixing the flour while she watched the two children. Because of the consistency, it ended up being more of a cake.

I put it in the oven, and after almost an hour, Mom looked at it.

"Catherine, that thing didn't rise." She snatched the dishcloth from the chair. "It's bubbling," she said as she reached in to grab the edge of the pan.

She laid the bread pan on the table, and we both stared at it. When it simmered down, I stuck my finger in the boiled batter and tasted it.

"Mom," I said as she stared at me expectantly. "This is awful sweet."

She stuck her finger in the pan and brought the white mixture to her lips. She sat down and shook with silent laughter. "For the love of God, I brought over the icing sugar."

We laughed about that mistake for years. The next day, she brought the "other" white flour, as she called it, and I made a dense cake for Mary with it.

I brought Mary for several check-ups to the Janeway over the next year. After twelve months, they told us that Mary's celiac was gone and she could return to normal eating.

The children, bright blessings in our lives, continued to come. It was October 21, 1958. I had been at Aunt Annie's for more than a week when the pains of labour on Francis started. Mary and Little Eddy were in North Harbour with my mother, and I was in St. John's waiting, somewhat impatiently, to go in the hospital.

Big Eddy would soon be home for the winter from the lumber woods in Badger, and I'd be happy enough to get home and see him. After he being gone since March, I wanted to get down to living a normal life, if only for a few months now that Mary was on the mend.

Aunt Annie was a fine hostess. Her children and grandchildren filled the house, but she made room for me. There was no grandeur about her, and anyone who stayed there had to pitch in. I didn't mind because it passed the time. She was like a second mother to me.

Before we got to have a mug-up in the morning, she had to call the taxi to come and get me.

"I'm sure glad it's not last January," my cousin Nellie said.

I laughed. "I'm sure you were embarrassed when the police came and got us."

"It wasn't when they come and got us, it was when they brought me back," she said. "Oh, the talk of the neighbours when I got out of the police car at eleven that night."

I laughed again before a labour pain laid siege to me. I grimaced as Aunt Annie brought my bag from upstairs.

"I could have gotten that," I said as I reached to take the bag from my aunt.

"I'm sure you could. Get out of here now before that baby is born in the kitchen," she said. "I don't want to have to clean up a mess." She smiled as she handed me the bag.

A short time later, I was at the Grace General Hospital, and Francis, named after my father and my deceased brother, was born. At first I was relieved to have it over with, but something wasn't right. The doctor and the nurses began to whisper, and the baby was kept out of sight from me.

I asked several times if he was all right. The nurse tried to comfort me, but I knew by her eyes that something was wrong. I became frantic. They allowed me to see him for a moment before he was rushed off by ambulance to the Janeway.

I gasped at the sight. The only way I can describe him was that his feet were turned wrong side out. There was nothing but two balls, like clenched fists, at the end of his legs. I went home a week later without him.

Visiting the Janeway with Mary over the coming months, I got to spend time with Francis. Not much, but enough to hold him on occasion. He had several operations. I'd get notified via a telegram that he was having surgery, or that he was doing well. I wouldn't get a message that he could come home until he was almost ten months old.

I'll never forget going in to get him and he was afraid of me. He cuddled up to the nurse and cried, not wanting to come with me. He wanted to stay with the nurses because they were all he knew. It broke my heart when he struggled and cried to get back to them. I was five months pregnant at the time.

Neil came along in November that year. He had something wrong with his feet and was taken away to the Janeway like Francis the year before. This time, the doctors just needed to snip a tendon on the instep of both his feet. Before I left St. John's, I was able to bring him home. We settled in for a winter with all hands under the same roof that year.

By spring of any year, there wasn't much to eat in the house. Eddy snared rabbits or would shoot a saltwater bird to keep us going. If anyone had a cow to kill, we'd have a few roasts. We had vegetables in the cellar from hard work in the gardens the year before, but by March these would be getting scarce as well. Times were hard more often than anything.

Every now and again, my sister May and her husband, Cecil, came from St. Mary's to see Mom and Dad in North Harbour and would take the road to see us in John's Pond. One day, I'd started to make soup on the only thing we had in the house, a salt beef bone, when I saw their car pull in.

I wished that I had more to offer them than the vegetable soup. I had bread that I'd baked the day before out of the last of our flour. Though not much, it would do. There was no grandeur about either of them, but they'd be welcomed at our table, grandeur or not.

That visit, they didn't stay long and were quickly on their way. I was peeling turnip for the soup when I heard the car again. Cecil called to Eddy to help him with a few boxes, and May came back inside.

I could have cried when I saw what they brought. They'd gone to Tom Ryan's store in North Harbour and bought staples like flour, butter, meat, tin milk, custard, tin fruit, and so much more. They brought in box after box of groceries.

I hugged May, that's all I could do. She didn't ask nor expect anything. I didn't know how I'd ever make it up to her for her kindness, but I hoped someday I could return the generous act. It wasn't the only time that she'd bring us groceries in the coming years. Each time she'd show up when it was desperately needed. Later that spring, Eddy left again for Badger, and that made it easier to fill the pantry for the winter.

In November, while Eddy was still away, I was back at St. Clare's again. This time, Richard was born. Similar to Francis, Richard was whisked away to the Janeway. His feet were severely clubbed; you couldn't recognize a foot at the end of his leg, either. I returned to John's Pond without him; my heart was broken.

That year in September, Mary started grade one. She had to walk the few miles to the south side of North Harbour to attend the one-room school. Me and Eddy talked about the distance. Mary was still poorly and found it difficult to get up the hill on the road, and especially the steeper incline on the way back. He wasn't having that.

People from the government were going around to small places like John's Pond and trying to get everyone to leave. They offered money, but nobody in John's Pond would sign to relocate. We were the only ones who wanted to go at that time.

We talked about a house on the north side of North Harbour, where Mom and Dad lived. We were going to a wedding there later that month, and Eddy said he would ask the owner, one of my cousins who'd moved to Placentia a few years prior, about selling it. We came to learn at the wedding that the house nearest my parents had been sold the month before to a Brewer family from Placentia Bay.

Another cousin had an old house near the church; we bargained for that, and Eddy bought it for $500. The Welfare Office gave him $600 to move. Eddy came home from the lumber woods early that year. By the summer, we were living in North Harbour, north side, settled into the old house. We brought Richard home to North Harbour. He was six months old at the time.

Eddy started work on the house in John's Pond. He took it apart, board by board, marking each one with its location by room, numbering them sequentially, and stacking piles to be brought over to North Harbour.

Seb Walsh had a big truck that was used to carry freight back and forth to the store. Eddy hired him with the remaining money for moving to bring the lumber to our yard. He went to work reassembling the house.

Marg came to stay with the children while I helped Eddy. In the new house, I puttied all the old holes on the clapboard on every bit of the house. If I couldn't reach them from the ground, I'd get out through the top windows onto the scaffold Eddy made and fill all the holes before it was painted. It was a lot of work, and we did it almost all ourselves.

Margaret Collins, Marg to me, had been dating my brother Dick since shortly after our wedding. She'd been teaching school in North Harbour the year we were married and met my brother when he came home for the occasion. They were married a year or so later and were building a house near my mother and father less than a mile from ours.

Marg quickly became my best friend. When Eddy and Dick were away, she often brought her youngsters to the house and stayed with me for weeks on end. I loved her company, and I didn't know it at the time, she was to become my saviour in many ways.

Larry was born eighteen months after Richard. He was diagnosed with a severe form of epilepsy after turning blue several times as a baby. He spent months in the hospital, and I made at least two trips a week with him to the cottage hospital in Placentia, if not more, when he'd have a seizure. It was trial and error with medication, and by the time he was settled on a kind that kept the seizures manageable, I'm sure I had made a thousand trips back and forth to the doctors if I'd made one.

Ida was born almost two years later. She was the first to be born in Placentia Cottage Hospital. She was so big that the baby scales couldn't weigh her. They brought her to the kitchen and came back and told me that she was fourteen pounds. Later I would come to learn that I most likely had gestational diabetes. However, though it might have been the case, it was undiagnosed. There were no more big babies after her.

Sharon came along almost eighteen months later, in February, and thankfully, she was all right. The next year, Harold was born in August, and I was happy to say he was healthy. Barry was born the next October. He, too, would have club feet like Francis and Richard. I came home without him. He was released about six months later with huge plaster casts on his feet.

5

The Trials and Tribulations
of This World

Meanwhile, Mary had become sickly again and was hospitalized multiple times. Francis, Richard, and Barry required visits to the hospital several times a year. Larry had to go to Placentia Hospital once and twice a week in order to try and control his seizures.

It was constant appointments and continually something to take the little bit of money we had. With Eddy away, I had to go by myself most of the time while Mom or Marg stayed with whoever I could leave home.

One time, Francis, Neil, and Richard had orthopaedic appointments with Dr. Shapter at the Janeway Children's Hospital in St. John's. Mom said she'd come and stay with Mary and Little Eddy because I was home with the children by myself while the senior Eddy was working and staying in the lumber woods in Badger.

I asked my cousin Paul to bring us to Colinet in the morning, and we met the taxi there around 5:00 a.m. at Lundrigan's. Lundrigan's was the taxi hub in the area. Another gentleman was going out, too, so he travelled with us from North Harbour and shared the first part of the fare.

There was quite a crowd that morning going to St. John's. The man with us got in the back by the door, I got in beside him with the three children. Two men were already in the front with the driver after coming from Placentia. The taxi picked up a woman and two children in Mount Carmel, and they came out with paper bags, and I groaned as I knew the children got carsick. The three got in the back with us. Another man got in the front shortly after. The last pickup that morning was a woman in St. Catherine's. She got in and lay across the three men in the front. The car was full.

The two oldest sat on each leg while I held Richard in my arms for the two-hour trip. The kids next to us threw up all the way out, making the air sickly in the warm car.

By the time people were let off at their destinations, we were dropped to the Janeway around 8:30 a.m. for a 9:00 a.m. appointment. The waiting room filled up for Dr. Shapter's clinic, and the receptionist began calling patients in. By noon the children were hungry and began to cry despite my trying to keep them quiet. We waited there until the end of the clinic at 5:00 p.m. We still hadn't been seen by the doctor, nor had any of us had anything to eat or drink. The late taxi came for us, and we had no choice but to go home again, getting there around 8:00 p.m. that evening. I got a loan of the additional fare from the store so we could go back the next day.

The taxi was full again. We returned to the clinic and were seen at the last appointment at around 4:45 p.m. The taxi came and we weren't ready, so he left us in St. John's. We were finished well after five o'clock, so I walked from the Janeway with the three children in tow the three miles to Aunt Annie's on Cochrane Street. Everyone was hungry, thirsty, and crying, and I almost felt like sitting down and bawling with them.

Aunt Annie was welcoming no matter the hour. She was mad that I hadn't gone there the night before, too. She fed us and gave us a bed, and we got the early taxi home the next day. It was a steady gait of going back and forth to the hospital. Several times we were left in St. John's, but every time, the receptionist would leave us till last. She came out of the office and looked right at me and then called somebody else. I had the feeling I was somehow beneath her standards.

After seven or eight times of this kind of treatment, I wrote a letter to Dr. McGrath, our Member in the House of Assembly. I told him what was happening and that I often came home without being seen despite having an appointment. I told him how far we had to travel and that it was quite costly.

I had the letter ready to post, but I couldn't find five cents in the house to get a stamp. I saw Dick coming up the road and shouted out to him from the window to ask if he had the price of the stamp. He did and took the letter and mailed it.

I regretted doing that after it was gone. Then I figured and partially hoped I'd be ignored. But Dr. McGrath wrote me back. He told me it wouldn't happen to me again. He said I would have priority from then on. He was right. Next time the three of the boys had an appointment, Eddy happened to be home and came with us.

When we got out of the taxi at the Janeway, Eddy wouldn't pay the driver. He told him that he'd pay when he got back to Colinet and not before so the driver wouldn't leave us.

I was embarrassed, even though Eddy was right. I wouldn't have said anything and would have just paid him. When we went in to the clinic, there was a different receptionist. We got in to see the doctor before ten and were able to get the early taxi home. Eddy paid both fares when we got to Colinet.

The next trip in, Dr. Shapter advised that Francis needed surgery.

"You'll have to leave him here for about ten days," he said.

"When will he get in?"

"Whenever there's a bed available. I'm sure your friend Dr. McGrath will get him in quickly," he said without looking up from the paper he was filling out.

"I'm sure he will," I said as my face reddened.

His hand paused for a moment, then continued writing. Shortly after, he explained what needed to be done. Then he went to check on bed availability. There was room for him that night, and the surgery was scheduled for the next day.

Francis was only six then. He went on with the nurse and didn't look back. He didn't cry or anything, he was so used to being in there. I took the other two and went home. Two weeks later, I was trading Francis for Richard. One came out and one went in. Richard was used to the operations on his feet as well.

On the way home, I was sitting next to the driver with Francis in my arms. He had casts on up to his hips with a metal bar separating them about the ankles. For the entire trip, Francis would look at me and then reach over and try to grab the wheel. I was sick and tired of saying "Francis" between gritted teeth and taking his hand away from the driver. He was a little devilskin, I supposed because he was spoiled in the hospital.

Francis adjusted to the casts and was able to get around pretty good despite the heaviness on his legs. Richard came home two weeks later with casts to his knees. Neither of them looked for extra care or attention; they fitted in as if they were no different than the others who had no leg or feet issues.

This scenario became routine over the years. Neil, thankfully, only had one surgery on his foot to straighten it. The snip when he was born had released the tension and only left him with the one cast for a little while. But he still had to go for checkups, although less frequently than the other two. Francis must have had fifty surgeries, the last one when he was fifteen. Richard had about thirty, and his last one was when he was ten. By then, Barry was born with the same club feet issue, and it was a repeat of sorts. He followed the same path as the other two with full and half leg casts, special boots, and bars between the boots. We had several sets of crutches at the house all the time.

The priest, Father Purcell, came in one day after Mass. It was very rarely that we missed a service, so he knew something was going on. This time, all hands had the measles. One of the young ones had been exposed at the hospital and brought it home. He said that the only thing he could compare the scene to was the Shea ward at the old General in St. John's. There were bodies bedded down everywhere in the kitchen and dining room so that I could keep watch on them all at once.

Barry was the only one that time who never got infected; he was in Placentia in the hospital when everyone else was sick. Mass contagions were common at the house. One of the children would bring home some kind of legacy from the hospital and infect the works of them.

With Eddy away most of the time, it fell to me to tend to whatever was on the radar at the time. I'd ease the suffering as best I could. I did what I had to do no matter how hard it was. I didn't think about it, just took one day and one child at a time in order to get through it.

6

The Deathly Things
That Do Not Kill Us

Barry was only home a few months when, after several trips to doctors in Placentia and in St. John's, I was told I had to have a hysterectomy. I'd been in a bad way since he was born. My iron was low to non-existent, as the doctor put it, and the only cure was surgery.

On November 28, 1970, I got a taxi from Aunt Annie's to go to the Grace Hospital. I'd left the youngsters home with their father. Mom said she'd visit in the day and do some chores, and Mary, who had turned sixteen by then, was there after school. Eddy was used to cooking for a crowd in the lumber woods, so they wouldn't starve. I was expected to be back home on December 12, and between us all, we'd make it through Christmas. I wasn't worried.

The surgery went well, according to Dr. Daly, the intern I'd met before in Placentia and who I'm sure had saved Mary's life. I had to stay in bed at the hospital for the two weeks and then could go home. The doctors told me my iron would level off in a month or so and I'd feel better with more energy than I had the entire year before. I was anxious to get home, because decorating had commenced at the hospital and Christmas music echoed through the halls, reminding me that I had much to do.

I was excited to finally get released, and my cousin Cecil Dalton (Aunt Annie's son) drove me home. He wouldn't take any money from Eddy when we got there. He had a cup of tea and wished us a Merry Christmas as he was heading out the door. This was one of the many kindnesses Cecil did over the years.

Eddy had baked bread. There were eight or ten pans of it with buns up on the table. The house smelled of home, and I didn't realize how I had longed for it. The youngsters were excited and chattering and hugging me before I got through the door despite warnings from my mother for them to be careful. It was good to be home. I quickly became tired that evening after the long drive and went to bed as soon as the littlest ones were squared away and tucked in.

The next morning, I woke in a haze. I couldn't clear my eyes nor keep them open. Pain was pulsing through me as I tried to get up. I heard the sounds of the day downstairs and thought it odd that everyone would be up so early. The clock on the table by the bed said it was past ten. It couldn't be. Confusion took over. I believed I was dreaming.

I rolled over, intent on getting up. My body was heavy and pulling me back. I felt the cold dampness of the mattress on my arm and hip, and I tried to sit up. My hand was sticky. Tentatively, I held it up in front of me. It was red. I pulled back the top sheet and swung my legs out over the side of the bed. The whole print of my frame was outlined on the bottom sheet by blood.

I shouted for Eddy and heard a racket on the stairs. I teetered as the bedsprings creaked beneath me. Eddy burst through the door, took one look, and backed up. He shouted for Francis or Eddy to go get Imelda.

Imelda was my first cousin who lived in the house on the other side of the graveyard from us. She was the go-to when anything medical was wrong. She had no nurse training but had a calmness about her in times of trouble. She'd bandaged more than one wound since we'd moved to North Harbour.

Eddy tried to get me out of the bed and had me standing when Imelda got there. She swiftly pulled off my nightdress and pulled some clothes on me. There was no time to clean me up. I could barely stand as the two of them guided me down the stairs. Eddy was in the front to take my weight in case I fell.

I must have been losing time, because before I knew it, one of the Bonias was there. He had a car and was going to bring me to Placentia Hospital. I couldn't stand. The youngsters were crying, and Eddy was trying to keep them back.

Imelda got Little Eddy to take the mattress off the daybed and put it in the back seat of the car. Two or three more men showed up, and between them all, they got me into the back seat. Droplets of blood followed my path from the bedroom to the car.

We had to go to the store first, because we had no money home and Eddy wouldn't go without something in case we were stuck. An older man was there and came out to speak to me to see how I was. Though I should have, I didn't know him, I was that far gone.

Imelda was in the middle in the front, Eddy pushed in beside her, and I was lying on the mattress. The freezing rain had started just as we left. It became slippery quickly; the driving conditions turned treacherous as we sped in the dirt road to the cottage hospital.

I was in and out of consciousness on the way. Imelda shouted out to me and at me, "Catherine, Catherine, can you hear me?" I'd mumble an assent and drift off again. She kept it up the whole way.

In Placentia Hospital, Eddy ran in to get help. Within minutes I was being hauled out onto a stretcher and pushed inside. Nurse McGrath met us at the top of the ramp. The first thing she did was call the priest. He came, and I was given last rites as part of the traditional Catholic sacraments for the dead and dying. The doctor assessed me and determined they couldn't do anything else for me there. I had to be rushed to St. John's in an ambulance.

There was only one available, which had already been called for another lady who was having a troubled labour. Since neither of us could wait, they stacked two of us inside. She was in the top rack, and I was in the bottom. Fear she was going to fall kept me alert.

We pulled in to the doors at the Grace Hospital ninety minutes later. Dr. Daly met me in emergency. He said, "Mrs. Linehan, you'll damn well be healed when you leave the next time." I was rushed into surgery within minutes. That was December 13, and it would be the last of February the next year before I'd see home again.

That time spent in the hospital was hard on me. I was confined to the bed and wasn't allowed out. Only for Cecil came to see me several times a week, and Ben Power, who was from North Harbour but working in St. John's at the time, I believe I would have lost my mind.

Ben came in after being home on the weekends, and he'd tell me news from the place. He'd bring word from Eddy about how everyone was doing.

I was lonesome, to say the least, and I didn't think my mind could stand the isolation. I was weaker than I'd ever been. To tell the truth, I was afraid I wouldn't get back home or that I would get home in the state I was in and wouldn't be able to cope with simple family things that I took for granted.

I celebrated Christmas there. I had a turkey dinner delivered to my room and listened to the music in the hall. That made it even harder, but I made the best of it. I was so used to the busyness of Christmas, and now, being bedridden, it was hard to deal with. I imagined Eddy not having anything for the children and them all being disappointed. I had no way to find out how he'd managed.

New Year's Eve I watched the fireworks through the window and prayed I'd soon be home, though I feared otherwise. I didn't think I was improving.

Thoughts that the children would forget me weighed heavily on my mind. It was a desperate time for me both physically and mentally.

Two months later, I was released. I never really knew what happened other than just about bleeding to death. All I knew was that I nearly perished and would have abandoned ten children to the care of their father. But I didn't and had gotten through the rough days.

Though I got home, I still had a lot of mending to do. I needed help at home, and Mary took on a lot of the caring for the small ones. I had no energy. I was tired all the time, and it took me almost two months just to get the strength and will to attempt going outside.

It was in May before I was able to walk, with great effort, as far as my parents' house. My father saw me coming over the hill one day and said to my mother, "I believe that's Catherine." They were so happy to see me out again that they both met me on the road and walked with me into the house. I was coming back to life.

I happily settled back into the machine of living after more than a year of misery. Along with bread, my home routine included the laundry. Three or four of the smaller ones were bedwetters. It was nothing to have two or three lines of clothes out and bread baked before noon each day.

It was hard work, but some days I'd drop the dishcloth and go play soccer with the children. I enjoyed the running around and kicking the ball to take my mind off the wringer washer and the drudgery of keeping house. In the winter, I'd go out and play hockey on the road with the crowd. I loved to hear the laughter and gaiety. It reminded me of being young and carefree.

Mary was the first to leave home. When she was in grade nine, she went to school in Mount Carmel because the one-room school did not offer the senior high courses she required to graduate. She boarded over in Mount Carmel and spent the weekends home.

She complained about her tooth on several occasions and needed to see the dentist. I made an appointment for her in Placentia, where the dentist ended up pulling the tooth. The next morning, Ida screamed for help up in their room. When I got there, Mary was covered in blood, and so were the pillow, sheets, and quilts. Eddy helped me get her down the stairs, and she wasn't able to stand up. She was staggering and groggy. Imelda came, and we got somebody in the harbour with a car to take us to Placentia. Mary was anemic and had very little iron most of the time, and now, very little blood. She was kept in hospital and given transfusions to stabilize her.

After a few weeks, we were told that her celiac disease was back. Since this was about fifty years ago, there was not a lot known about the disease, and the fact that it hadn't gone away contributed to Mary's many hospital stays in her youth.

Neil complained of being cold all the time. It could be the hottest day out, and he had on long sleeves or a coat. He couldn't be warmed. He complained of a pain in his back and a pain in his side. I brought him to Placentia more times than I could count before the doctors said it was his appendix causing the trouble. They booked him for surgery in Placentia. Neil was thirteen.

I left him at the hospital and went home. He'd have the operation within a day or so and had to stay in for another week. We got word a few days later that his surgery was done, and both myself and Eddy went in to see him the next day.

He was out on the ward when we got there, and he wasn't feeling very good. We thought it was a post-surgery thing. There was a man in the bed next to him from Branch. He was a Nash. He told us that he stayed up all night watching Neil because he was sure the young fellow was dying. He said he was really afraid for him and called the nurses several times during the night.

We talked to the surgeon about it, and he didn't seem too concerned. Neil developed a fever after that, and it was hard to treat. He was kept in the hospital for a few weeks, all told.

Neil was no sooner home than he was complaining about a bad back again. It came and went. He was usually cold. He was able to run cross-country meets with the school some days, and others the pain was too bad.

A new doctor came to Placentia and opened a clinic away from the hospital. I took Neil to him a few times when he was in more pain than usual. The doctor ordered an X-ray to see what was going on. I brought Neil over to the hospital and went back with the X-ray as he'd asked. The doctor looked at it and couldn't find one of Neil's kidneys.

Neil went to St. John's to the Janeway for surgery within a few days. His kidney had rotted away over the years, which was why he constantly had the sore back. It had probably never been his appendix at all. Once he had the operation, his back got better. It was major surgery to have, but he recovered well.

Going between Placentia Hospital and the Janeway Hospital became a routine. It was also costly. We had no vehicle and always had to hire somebody to go. Jos was good to us at the shop. If I needed money, she gave it to me and marked it down. Our groceries were also marked down to pay at the end of the month or pay later. We had two bills, one for immediacies like groceries, school supplies, clothing, and one for urgencies, where the medical trips came into the picture. There were many times I didn't think later would ever come. The Baby Bonus cheques were signed over, but it didn't cover what we owed. Eddy's cheques kept the lights on, and anything to spare went to constant fares to and from appointments or emergencies.

7

The Ups and Downs of Normal

Eddy spent a lot of time in the country hunting seasonal game—moose, rabbits, and partridges—in the gardens growing vegetables, or farming sheep and raising a cow each year, mostly for the table. He'd sell small game or berries to make extra money. Bakeapple money went to school outfits and supplies.

Though Eddy claimed the sheep were his, I'd often beg to differ. There was nobody put as many terms, and not good terms, down on top of sheep as what I did, especially in the spring of the year. They were plain and simple, hard work. Most of it, Eddy knew nothing about.

The sheep had to be sheared in April or May, and Eddy wasn't home most of that time to do it. Even if he was, the job was left to me. Only for I needed the wool so badly, I'd let them go all summer in their woolly coats. But times were hard, and winter would come again, and the youngsters needed mittens, hats, and socks.

There was a big scissors in the house, and that was used for shearing. I'd get Eddy's stone and sharpen it as much as I could before I'd tackle the real job. When the boys were old enough, there were times I'd get them to help me corner one of the sheep, and other times I'd rig up a fence to catch them. Once I was close enough to grab hold of it, I'd flip the sheep on its side on the ground, holding down its neck with an elbow, and start cutting. The sheep struggled and bawled as I snipped away. Then I'd have to turn them over to do the other side.

If Eddy happened to be home, he'd rig up a table so that it was easier on me than kneeling in the grass. He could lift them up for me. But either way, my fingers ached, blistered, and bled, and my arms were limp by the time the last of the twenty were done. Not many of them escaped without a nick or two, but it couldn't be helped.

Once they were sheared, I had to wash the wool and bag fifty-pound flour sacks full to send to Nova Scotia to the woollen mill. I'd hope for enough yarn to make do for the winter, and though I washed and picked it, I was consistently paid as if it were unwashed. I'd be put out by that and swear I wasn't going to wash it the next year, but I'd give in and do it.

Anything to do with the wool in general was a yearly task I dreaded the most of anything I had to do to get by. In second place would be the work that went with making hay for them for the winter. But in the fall of the year, the butcher came, the lambs were culled, and the few dollars Eddy received for them made up for the pains of the spring. The sheep money helped get us through the winters.

The horse was there for hauling wood, and if Eddy had a good year working, he'd get a calf to rear. When it was big enough in the summer, the cow would graze on the cliffs and meadows in the abandoned community we knew as Cape Dog. Eddy would walk the cow out and go back for it in the fall.

One year, he went back but the cow was gone. He hunted for it for a few days and found the carcass near the meadows. The cow had been shot what was probably months before. Nothing was touched on it, so he didn't know if somebody had done it for sport or had mistaken it for a moose. It was a big loss for us, but Eddy didn't mention it after. The next year, he kept the cow home.

That one was our last; she was named Flossy. Flossy didn't like being milked and often kicked at me or jammed me in the wall of the pound. Eddy used to have to go to the stable with me to keep the cow quiet enough to milk. He'd hold her around the neck, and if she made a move on me, he'd give her a knock or a squeeze to keep her still. When he wasn't around, I'd have a stick to keep her back. I wasn't afraid of her, but I wasn't fond of her, either.

In the spring, Flossy became aggressive. The kids would get off the bus, and she'd charge the gate. Eddy ended up tying her to the light pole on a short rope so she couldn't reach the lane. The children were afraid of her and would run into the house crying that Flossy was mooing at them. Although they hated Flossy, when they came home and Flossy was gone, they wouldn't eat the pot of stew because they were convinced that Flossy was in the pan. She was.

So that was the end of cows. Eddy got hens after that. Another thing for me to tend while he was away working. But every little bit helped, and having eggs every day didn't go astray in our burgeoning household.

Another opportunity came when road construction between North Harbour and Branch began. There were no bridges on the bigger rivers, so many of the workers were looking for places to stay during the week. Although we had a houseful, we made room and took in two boarders from Branch. Our place was bursting at the seams.

Thankfully, they didn't care about the crowded quarters, nor did they complain. I'd cook their supper and make their lunch. They'd stay all week and return to Branch on the weekend. We needed the money, and they were no trouble. When I was cooking for twelve, fourteen was not much different. I'd added a few pans of bread to my daily baking ritual and extra potatoes in the pot at suppertime.

Another year, Eddy took on a guiding trip for US Army folks from the Argentia Naval Base. He struck up a friendship with Americans, Lloyd Olds and his wife, Bonnie. The Olds family came to the house often in the coming few years before Lloyd was stationed elsewhere. They brought something each visit, and each one was as good as or better than any Christmas we could ever provide. One spring they brought bikes for the kids; in the summer there were toys or board games. On rainy days the children would be hunched over a game of Life, or Payday, or any number of other games that came from the base.

We spent many hours with the Oldses playing Yahtzee. That became our favourite game. The house would be in chaos, kids everywhere, both ours and theirs, but they never seemed to mind the much simpler life we lived.

The October Barry was born, they sent me baby clothes and several cases of disposable diapers. But Barry spent his first several months in the hospital and would have been too big for them when he got home. So, without need for them, I gave them to Marg for Joey, who was born a month later. I wouldn't get to enjoy my first chance at "convenience" after all.

In the winter, Eddy made slides out of barrel staves that came from Argentia as well. There would be fifteen or twenty of them leaning up against the stable for anyone to take for a ride. The Oldses brought out a monstrous size of a metal slide that only several of the biggest of the bunch of kids could pull up the hill. I was kind of afraid of that one. It sat about eight kids comfortably, two side by side. But when the thing took off at the top of Soaker's Path, there would be fourteen and fifteen aboard. I'd watch through the window when the shouts and hollers started, and if they could make the turn at the bottom of the path, within moments they'd be coming through the back gap and down the hill. The slide would take air a couple of times on snow ramps the boys would build and end up in the river that was piled high with snow, which formed a brake against the fence. A few of the stragglers who chose the stave slides would come down the hill, and they would all mash up together. Nobody ever suffered a broken limb, so it was all in good fun, but I held my breath every time I watched them race down that hill.

The Oldses brought barrels, boxes, and garbage bags of clothes the likes of which I hadn't seen before. I managed to get a few things for myself out of it. But more often than not, I took apart slacks, and using the old Singer sewing machine, I sized them smaller to fit the girls. I shared with Marg what we didn't need and she could use. We'd trade back when one of the boys or girls outgrew something in one family or the other. Out of the scraps I pieced together quilts and re-topped old and torn bedding. It was a tremendous help and even a respite when we needed it.

It was a time when nothing was wasted. There was no room for that in the struggle of poverty.

8

The Art of Growing Up

After Larry finished grade two, the one-room school closed in North Harbour, and everyone had to take the bus to Mount Carmel. Ida was the first in the family not to go to school in the harbour. There was no more coming home at noon; it was packed lunches from then on.

When Barry started school a few years later, Mary had just graduated and went to trades school in Placentia that September. Barry was also the first to attend kindergarten in the family. That was new in the schools from the year before, which meant Harold went one year to grade one and Barry went the next to kindergarten and Harold to grade two. We had nine children on the bus at the same time that year.

That first day Barry went to school, it was also the first time that all hands were gone, and the house was empty. Marg and Jos were in the same boat as me. All our children were in school for the morning, with their youngest being Barry's age. Between us, we made a plan to pick blueberries. This was a luxury for me to be able to go with the women without a trail of children behind me. But we also weren't familiar with the half-day schedule and didn't know exactly when the kindergarten class would be home.

We were in the berry patch having a chat and picking away at the blueberries when Marg looked at the time. We figured the boys would soon be home, so we headed out of the woods. By the time we came out the path behind the shop, Kenny was waiting for his mother. I panicked because Barry was the stop before Kenny. Marg made a dash down the road to get Joey, and I ran up the road.

When I made it to the house, I heard Barry sobbing on the doorstep. He was all right but had gotten a scare. Poor child, his first time in school and then came home to an empty house. My heart sank, and I swore I'd never do that again. I brought him into the house and gave him whatever he wanted for the rest of the day.

When the family all got home on the bus in the evenings, usually around four, our yard would fill with children. We were the midway point in the harbour and became the easiest place to meet. There was nothing to see thirty or forty children out playing soccer or baseball. Every year, Eddy rigged up a set of swings from the woodpile with rope from the stable he'd had for the horse.

Eddy landed a job as a river guardian. Though it was not as much pay, it meant he was home almost every evening. He'd drive a dirt bike supplied by the province to and from work on North Harbour River or out to Branch. Though it wasn't really ours, it was the only vehicle we'd ever had. I liked that Eddy was home. It was good to have him around to share in some of the outdoor chores.

Our first and only family vacation, as the children called it, came the next summer. There was a cabin on the banks of North Harbour River where Eddy would spend a night or two if the salmon were running. It was to guard against poachers when the salmon were most vulnerable.

For us, going there was only a day trip, but it was a big deal, being out of the ordinary. I made bread and jam sandwiches, and Eddy had brought extra tea and mugs when he left the day before. We got a ride in the back of a truck as far as the river, found the path to the cabin, and hiked in. It wasn't that far, because we could see the roof from the road. We spent the day there, the kids running around and playing in a not so familiar place. Ida got stung by a bumblebee when she was picking berries, and I had to get black bog to take the sting out of it.

Overall, it was a fun day. When evening came, we got back to the road at the scheduled time to get a drive to the house. Eddy wanted me to ride down on his bike, but I was afraid. The children encouraged me to go with him, so, despite better judgment, I did.

The truck went on with the youngsters, and I got on the back of the bike. Eddy started off, and I screamed. He stopped and waited for me to settle. I made an offer to get off and walk home but told him to go on again. Every few feet, I'd scream and shout to get off. I was terrified. Eddy was going so slow that he had to keep his feet on the ground, but it didn't matter to me, I was afraid. That's the way we went home, and what should have taken about ten minutes took almost an hour.

Eddy was patient and joked that he could have brought me home in the wheelbarrow quicker. It was my first and my last drive on that bike.

Our house became a central point in the harbour as the boys got older. Every one of mine had three or four others their age, or more, in North Harbour, and all their friends gathered to play. There'd be road hockey in the winter and soccer or softball in the summer. The place would overflow with children.

One year, they all decided to make a town in the woods behind the house. Over the next few years, there was an intricate set of trails cut out and a town complete with hospital, hotel, bank, and even a log cabin–type jail built across the entire ridge. They'd play sheriff and robbers, picking teams with one crowd as the good guys and another crowd as the bad. It was nothing to hear shouts and gales of laughter from the hill after school and on the weekends and most of the summer. All ages were included, and nobody was left out.

Just before dark, I'd go to the back door and shout for all hands to go home. There was never a back answer or a no; everyone streamed out of the woods and either in the house or out through the yard to go up or down the road to home.

Winter and summer were alike at our place. It was full there all the time, but I didn't have an ounce of trouble with anyone. Children came in to get warmed if they were cold, to get a slice of toast if they were hungry, or to rest if they were tired.

One year, we got a floor-model TV out on instalments in St. John's. On rainy days the place was full of kids, and you couldn't put your foot down in the living room because of bodies everywhere. But there wouldn't be a sound, as all hands would be attentive to the television.

Despite the hard times we went through as parents, and though the kids had their troubles with sickness, they also had lots of fun. They made good times out of nothing but imagination and a little bit of work.

After Mary took a secretarial course at the college in Placentia, she moved to and began working in St. John's. Eddy and Neil went to trade school to be electricians and were working each day in town with a local company. They came home in the night to North Harbour. Francis took civil engineering, and Richard studied and graduated from surveying technology at college in St. John's. They both got work with the Department of Transportation locally, and they lived at home, too.

The first year Richard was away in school, when he came home one weekend, he asked me if I could get him a pair of boots for Christmas. Then he asked me if Christmas could come early because the cardboard soles in his boots were constantly wet from leaks. I asked Mom for money, and I got him the boots the next week. Mom would often call for the boys to go down at the end of the month and give them a few dollars before they'd go back to school in St. John's.

While they were in college, or in Mary's case working in town, they brought home friends from all over the province. Every weekend the house was full to capacity with people from the Northern or Burin Peninsulas or the South Coast of the island. Our home became a home to many who were far away from theirs. There would be five or six to a bed and more on the floor upstairs. I never knew how many I had to feed on a Sunday, but it was often a bigger crowd.

Once the older ones were finished school and were set-tled into work, things started to look up. The boys would buy big items for the house, like a chesterfield set, a washer and dryer to replace the wringer washer and clothesline, a colour television to replace the black and white, and so many more things. They were generous and kind-hearted.

9

The Community Car

Francis got a job with the Department of Transportation as a civil engineer. With road construction in the area, and no office in the vicinity, he was asked if he'd mind working from home. Francis set up on the dining room table and conducted his business from there. The table wasn't a real piece of furniture but a sheet of plywood that Eddy had cut a foot off the width, put legs on, and that I'd painted brown. The piece that was cut off had been fashioned into an eight-foot-long bench, also painted brown, and rested against the wall. Chairs were all shapes and qualities and served their purpose.

People came and went; surveyors, drivers, and many more began to show up around noon. Francis would push back his rolls of paper and whatever instruments he was using, the men would sit around the table, and I'd get them tea. It was a busy place.

While he was working from home, Francis bought a light brown Chevy Malibu, the first vehicle to be owned in the household. Both his father and I were proud of him and happy to see a car in the yard.

On the weekends, the car never cooled. Francis and his buddies would be gone from Friday evening to Sunday evening. He'd come home to change or eat and then go again, sometimes taking his guitar. During the week, somebody would phone and ask Francis if they could have his car to bring their mother to Placentia, or to go to St. John's for something. Francis never said no. It was nothing for the car to be gone overnight. Nobody came in for keys; I don't know if the car had none or if the keys were usually in her.

Francis could never keep a cent of money. His father kept a $20 bill that Francis would borrow one week and give back to him the next when he got paid. Eddy would often joke that the only money he had in his wallet was Francis's twenty.

But no matter the demands on the car, if either myself or his father had to go anywhere or had appointments, Francis made sure the car was home so he could take us.

One day, Eddy asked me if I wanted to go in the country with him. He was going after rabbits, the snares were out, and he wasn't sure how many he'd get. I understood I was going along to help carry the rabbits if they were plentiful. I didn't mind getting out of the house for a few hours in the peace and quiet of the outdoors, so I was quick to agree.

Francis said he'd bring us out on the road, but because he was working and wouldn't know for sure when we'd be back, he offered to leave the car in a pit near where we'd pick up Eddy's snare trail. One of the Bonias came out behind us and took Francis back with him and would bring him back out later. The plan was that we could wait in the car, or he'd wait for us, whoever got there first.

After about an hour, the sky suddenly turned black. Eddy had four or five rabbits by then and had only hauled a quarter of the snares.

"We better get under cover of the trees," Eddy said as he looked skyward. We veered toward a nearby thicket, when the skies opened and sheets of rain soaked us to the skin. The tree-line didn't give us much shelter, and the rain didn't look like it would let up.

"We better make our way out," he said. "We're wet any-way."

"Yes, we'll catch our death here," I said. The chill made me shiver in the wet clothes. We started for the road, heads down and silent. Three times I had to get Eddy to stop. I'd catch a tree or his arm for balance and pour the water from my short rubbers. The rain was so heavy, it was hard to see where we were going. We trudged along, taking well over an hour to get out. The rubbers were hard to walk in, the bogs sucking them down and the water filling them up. By the time we saw the road, we were almost upon it, the rain was so heavy.

It was nice to get on the hard surface of the road. I emptied my rubbers once more, and we beat it for the car. When we got to the pit, there was no vehicle.

"Did we come out in the right place?" I asked.

"Yes, this is where we got out. That's my marker there on the trail," Eddy said as he pointed to the piece of plastic bag tied on a raggedy little spruce on the embankment. The pit was small, and there was no place for the car to be, only right in front of us.

"We have to walk, that's all is to it," Eddy said as he fixed the straps of the knapsack he carried.

"Something must have happened," I said as fear washed over me.

"Now, Catherine, we'll find out when we get home."

We started out on the road, hoping somebody would come along. We'd gone about five or six miles when we walked out of the rain. I emptied my boots again; the wet socks were chafing my heels, and I knew I'd have blisters the next day. A fellow from Branch came along when we were nearly in reach of the harbour. He picked us up and wanted us to get in the cab, but we were waterlogged and said we'd be okay in the back of the truck.

At the house, there was no sign of Francis's car. I was getting tormented by then; all kinds of thoughts of what had happened were circling like buzzards in my head. Francis was at the table when we walked in.

"What happened to you? Where did you come from?" he asked.

I told him what happened. "Where's the car?"

"I don't know," he said.

"Didn't you see the rain? You could have sent somebody for us."

He shook his head and went to the door. "I had my head down and didn't notice."

Eddy lit the fire, and we got changed. I did have blisters.

"You're going to have neither car left, Francis, if you don't knock off what you're at."

He only nodded. The car showed up in the yard later that evening. I never asked if he knew who had it. There was no point in knowing.

A few weeks later, we were coming home from Placentia. It poured rain, and Francis turned on the wipers. They wouldn't work. He hooked shoelaces to them to get us home. He looked at me and grinned.

The next time we went to Placentia, coming out the dirt road, Francis stopped the car. He popped the hood and got out.

"What's wrong with her now?" I asked as he came around to my side.

"She's overheating. I need something to get water."

I heard the trunk slam, and he came back to the door again, empty-handed. I got out and rummaged in the back seat.

"There's nothing here," I said.

"Is that a shoe or a sneaker?" he asked as he pointed toward the floor.

"Yes, a sneaker, there's two of them here."

"Give me one," he said.

I looked at him under my eyes and handed him the sneaker through the window. Francis went around the car and down over the embankment. He came back moments later carrying water in the sneaker. I went around the front of the car and watched him pour the water into what he told me was the radiator. Three or four times he went over the bank and came back to pour the water.

"If anyone ever sees us," I said as I tut-tutted and shook my head at the situation.

We got back in the car and went for about fifteen minutes, when Francis stopped again. He grabbed the sneaker, popped the hood, and proceeded to fill the radiator. When he got back in, the two of us laughed. The next time he stopped, I got down in the ditch and handed him up the water. The sneaker was getting good use.

We stopped twice more before we got home.

"Who owns the sneakers?" I asked him. "They're not yours."

"I don't know. Must be one of the boys left them there."

"Well, they're going to get some fright."

The two of us laughed. There was no point getting mad with Francis, because he was as carefree as they came. He didn't have a care in the world.

10

Our Full House

Jer (Jeremiah) Bonia was a widower. His wife had died years before, and having had no children, he was sort of adrift in the community in his senior years. He spent his days smoking a pipe either at the store or visiting around the harbour. He lived with an older couple, and when they couldn't care for him any longer, he went to a boarding house in Holyrood.

Jos and Seb paid him a visit and found out he didn't like to be there. Jos heard me say that I would have taken Jer in. She phoned me and asked me if I'd do just that. I had a houseful of young ones, but they were all in school now, so I said yes. Jer was no trouble. He was quiet as an old dog.

Marg accompanied me the next day in Holyrood to take him home. He cried when he saw me and knew I was taking him back to North Harbour. There was another old woman there, who started to sob when she saw Jer going.

"Marg, we better get out of here or I'll be going home with Jer under one arm and Mrs. Young under the other."

I didn't know Mrs. Young, of course, but I had that kind of feeling just the same. She needed to be cared for, and that was what I was used to doing.

At home, the living room took up one half of the down-stairs, running back to front. Eddy chopped lumber by hand and barred it off to make a bedroom downstairs for Jer. We traded the dining room and the living room so that the stairs separated Jer from the TV in case there was any noise when he went to bed. With a few sheets of panelling, the room was up in a day.

Jer gave me money every month when he got his pension. This covered his room and board, but the first couple of months I spent what he gave me to fit him out with a winter coat, shirts, pants, and shoes.

He spent his days in the rocking chair smoking his pipe. He became part of everyday life, and the children treated him well. After a few years, Jer began getting on with foolishness about a political figure in the province named John Crosbie. Eddy and Francis used to torment him about Crosbie, and Jer would get clean off his head.

It was usually the same thing on repeat that started it every time. Little Eddy turned around in the chair and looked at Jer. That was all it took.

"Crosbie's taking Topsail Road," Jer used to say, his eyes fiery.

"No, he's not," Eddy would say, and that rose the racket for the next half-hour.

One day, Jer whipped out the cane and clobbered Little Eddy on the head. He deserved it, but I had to put my foot down then.

"I want no more talk of Crosbie. Do you hear me?"

"Crosbie's taking Topsail Road," he said again, his voice milder this time.

"I don't care if Crosbie takes the Island," I said. "I want no more talk of him here."

Jer nodded and looked at Little Eddy under his eyes. A few times after that, he shook the cane at him when he thought I wasn't looking but didn't utter Crosbie's name again. Eddy and Francis only laughed, and I warned the two of them to leave Jer alone. They listened when I was around, but I knew they didn't when I wasn't there.

Either way, Jer was harmless and well-fed. He loved being at the house despite the crowd. In his latter days there, he had trouble getting washed and dressed. I helped him, then, and got him up and ready for the day, every day. It was all quite predictable.

Then, on June 16, 1980, I woke when the air shifted the curtain on the window and brushed across my face. I heard the door downstairs. It didn't sound like the boys getting ready to go to work. I looked over Eddy's shoulder at the clock on the stand. It was just after five.

Who was up? Or who was in the house? I hopped out of bed and rushed to the window at the end of the hall not knowing what to expect.

It looked like Jer, but he was going too fast and was too straight and tall to be him. I shook my head to clear the confusion. I had to be seeing things, but when I looked again, I thought it was Jer.

I leaned out over the rail, and Jer's door was open. It had to be Jer, but at the same time, it couldn't be. I looked again to make sure I wasn't seeing things, but there was a man going out the lane toward the road. With the ocean just across the road, my heart went up in my throat. I ran across the hall and down the stairs. I peeked in Jer's room, and he was gone.

I didn't feel the gravel under my bare feet as I tore out the lane in my nightdress. I caught up with Jer at the gate.

"Jer, where are you going?" My tone was a cross between frightened and angry.

"I'm going to haul up my dory," he said as he struggled to open the latch on the gate.

"Your dory?" I questioned. "Jer, you don't have a dory." The last time Jer had fished was at least forty years previous.

"There's a storm coming, she'll be lost," he said as he fidgeted with the hook to get the gate unlatched.

"You're not going out there," I said. "You're dreaming. Go back to bed out of it."

He pushed on my hands to get me out of the way. But I held the gate. He was not getting by me. I couldn't believe that Jer was fully clothed and standing taller than normal, when only a few hours before I had to take off his clothes and put on his pyjamas.

"The dory will be lost," he said angrily. "She'll be lost."

"I'll look after the dory," I said with conviction. "Now, you go back to bed."

That seemed to quieten him. Jer nodded and carried on back up the lane as if he was satisfied the dory would be saved. He walked swiftly for a man who was normally hunched over and needed a cane to get around.

I followed him in. He was sitting on the edge of the bed trying to get off his shoes. I pulled them off him and helped swing Jer's legs back in the bed, this time clothes and all.

The next morning when I heard him stirring, I went in. I asked Jer what he'd gotten up for, but he didn't remember what had happened. Only because he was fully dressed did I truly believe it hadn't been me that dreamt it.

11

The Last of the Good Old Days

"How many are in Mary's room?" Eddy asked as he peeled away at the potatoes on the table.

"I saw five heads, and Sharon and Ida are in sleeping bags by the foot of the bed," I said as I came across the kitchen after coming down the stairs.

"What about over in Francis's room?" he asked and looked up, pausing with the half-peeled potato to stare at me.

"There's only one extra over there," I said.

Eddy counted the air with the tip of the knife. "Eighteen," he said.

I nodded.

"Is there enough beef on?" He paused in peeling once again, laid the knife on the table, and went to the stove, taking the cover off the pot. Steam wafted up around him before he bent over the boiler and counted with a nod the number of pieces. "Six big pieces. Do you think that's enough?"

"We're not feeding an army," I said.

"We want to have enough." He head-gestured for me to look in the boiler.

I sighed. He moved away still holding the cover over the pot. I stepped in and looked down.

"We'll make it enough. I don't think there's any left in the bucket." I moved toward the table and picked up the carrot peeler.

He took the long metal spoon and swirled it around, I supposed counting the salt meat pieces once again. "You're sure there's none left?"

"Positive," I said. "We'll have to send for a bucket sometime the week."

Eddy dipped the spoon in the water once again and tasted the broth. "That's a bit too salty. I'll change the water." He laid the cover on the counter and took the boiler off of the range. He poured the hot liquid down the sink, keeping an eye on how much he was dumping. Once the water drained out, he laid the boiler in the sink and turned on the tap.

The reddened coils on the damper spit the stray droplets when Eddy laid the boiler back. He replaced the cover and returned to the table.

"I want to have enough," he said. "Can't have anybody hungry."

Eddy had grown up in hard times. His mother died of the Spanish flu when he was a toddler, so he went to live with an aunt and uncle. By the time he was eleven, he was out working. He moved to Holyrood as a teenager, helping a family of Mac-Donalds with their farm. In his early twenties he went to Scotland in the Newfoundland Overseas Forestry Unit (NOFU) and stayed there working for the war effort for almost four years.

He was on his own nearly all his life, until he settled down with me when he was thirty-six. He'd seen poor times, and we'd seen poor times together, but he'd say as long as there was something to eat, that was the main thing.

We'd been feeding students from the College of Trades and Technology in St. John's who'd come home with Francis, Neil, or Richard, as well as friends of Mary's who came in with her on the weekends. We'd never know how many were going to wake up at the house on Sunday mornings. I'd have extra bread baked, and we'd have lots of vegetables for the pot to have enough.

Ours was a busy place on Saturday nights when all hands were trying to get ready for the dance at Dick's Riverview Lounge at the end of the Salmonier Line. Sunday mornings were only busy for the two of us because the first of the older ones wouldn't come down the stairs until just before noon. None of them that had darkened our doors up to then would have said a word to us if we'd called them early, but we left them alone, content in the sounds of the boiling pot and the steamed-up windows.

Larry was an early riser. He'd be up, have toast and tea, and be gone either up the road to Clem and Marie's or Ben Bonia's, or down to Mr. Vince Walsh's place. These were all seniors in the community, and Larry went there every day, Monday to Sunday, to help with whatever they wanted.

The two youngest boys, Harold and Barry, would be the next to come down, and then Sharon and Ida. I'd make them toast on the damper of the wood stove before they'd go about their day, outside if it was nice, in the living room if it wasn't. Jer would get up and dress and sit in the rocking chair, where he'd spend the day.

It was a routine we fell into gladly. Having eighteen or twenty was no more to us than having ten or a dozen, as we learned a long time ago. Eddy was of the same mind as I was on that. Neither of us cared as long as there was enough.

I scooped a bowl of flour from the barrel and began mixing up a molasses pudding and then a light raisin pudding. Eddy got the cloths ready once the dough was mixed. I'd scoop the bowl into the middle of the square of heavy yellowed cotton and bring up all the sides, twisting the ball tight. Eddy cut the string and wound it around between my fist and the top edge of the ball. Once it was tied, he'd take it and throw it in the pot with the now boiling beef. We'd repeat for the next one, and then, if I had the yellow split peas, we'd throw in a third pudding.

By the time the cabbage, turnip, carrot, and potato were added, the huge boiler would be overflowing. On days I didn't make the puddings, I'd make dumplings.

Mayhem started just before noon. We'd hear laughter and voices from the room first, then one of us would shout out from the bottom of the stairs when dinner was ready. Like a herd of elephants, they'd trample down the steps. Once the greetings were done, everyone would take a plate or a bowl, pick up what they wanted for dinner, and grab a seat around the table or on the chesterfields in the living room.

It was like that for three or four years. The faces sometimes changed, but the extra crowd was welcome. It was mostly friends from outports who were used to large families but, while in school, were too far away to go home except for Christmas holidays. We had nothing in the way of grandeur, but that wasn't what anyone was looking for.

Once dinner was finished, I didn't have to worry about a dish. They were cleaned and put away and the place tidied before anyone left to go back to St. John's with full bellies, several loaves of bread, a feed of leftovers for Monday, and shouts of, "We'll see you next weekend."

June 17 was a busy day. Barry had a part in the concert in the lower grades, and I went over with Jos and Seb and Marg. After that, all the rest of the children were invited to the school for awards night, so we came home, got something to eat, and went back again.

Harold was sitting next to me in the gym. He was worried and kept tapping me on the leg or the arm and saying, "I think I'm here by mistake." He believed he'd be in trouble for being there. Larry got ribbons and medals for high marks, Ida got trophies and ribbons for high marks and for sports. Sharon was called up several times for blue honours ribbons, medals, and trophies in cross-country, volleyball, and other gym events. All the while Harold sat next to me fidgeting and saying he was there by mistake.

By the time the grade sevens were called, several other kids were invited up, and Harold couldn't hold still in the chair. By and by, they called his name. He had received honours. Well, he sprang off the chair when they said Harold Linehan. He was so delighted. When he came back to his seat with the blue ribbon, he said, "Mom, I thought it was a mistake. I really did." His eyes were as big as saucers, and the smile was bursting his cheeks. He was so happy and shocked at making the honours list that it was the best part of the night.

The next day, June 18, came bright and sunny. It was a short day in school, the final day. When the children burst from the bus and roared into the house, there was pandemonium as the excitement for summer holidays had finally come. Once they settled down, they all went to their grandmother's with reports and told her how they did the night before. Mom gave them a few cents to get candy at the store.

Time was flying by. There were talks that Barry would be doing grade seven the next school year, at least do some of the courses. Harold would go to grade eight in the fall, Sharon to grade nine, and Ida to grade eleven. Larry was finished high school with all but the exams to do. They'd start the next day.

That evening, just before dark, Harold and Barry came up with the idea that they wanted to sleep in the tent that night since it was their holidays. The tent, a large canvas affair, was fine, but the poles had been cracked off a few years before. The older boys cut poles on the ridge when they were setting it up, but Neil said there were none and they'd have to ask me. It was too dark to go up in the woods to find poles that would suit what they needed.

"Wait until tomorrow night," I said. Their heads hung in unison for a moment before their red-freckled faces beamed up at me and smiled in agreement. They'd hold off on camping until the next night.

Life was full of promise.

Until it wasn't.

Part II

The Chasm

———————————

—————————

12

The Crippling Weight of What One Must Bear

I awoke on what I would later know was the worst day of our family's lives. Something had roused me. I sat on the side of the bed and listened. I turned to Eddy's timepiece and peered at it over the blankets that covered him. The grey of breaking daylight illuminated the neon green in the big and little hands and showed it was going for 5:00 a.m.

There it was again. A sound I didn't recognize. *Jer* was my first thought after chasing him a few nights before. I went to the same window again, but there was no sign of Jer. Then I doubled over the rail of the stairs and saw his room door was closed. I looked out the window again, but I couldn't see anyone or anything out of place. It wasn't time for the boys to be up for work, so that wasn't it.

The air around me felt unusually warm, almost hot. I heard a crackling noise. I thought it strange. I listened again, and sure enough it sounded like the fire was in. I went back to the bedroom, and Eddy was still there, the blanket moving slightly with each breath. It wasn't him gone to light the stove. I uttered words that I don't know where they even came from.

"Eddy. Eddy, I believe the house is on fire."

He bolted upright and swung his feet over the side of the bed. He grabbed his pants and hauled them on. "What? How do you know?"

"I heard crackling sounds. But I'm not sure."

He rushed out the door ahead of me, forgetting his glasses on the nightstand in front of the clock. Almost blind without them, he navigated the stairs by rote.

He was a step ahead of me as he rounded the corner from the bottom of the stairs into the living room. Little Eddy was asleep on the chesterfield.

Eddy poked him. "Were you cooking anything? Did you leave anything on the stove?"

Little Eddy stirred, and Eddy carried on into the kitchen and checked the electric range and the wood stove. He came back to me and Little Eddy. We both heard the noise now, but there was no smoke, nor any sign of fire. However, the room was unusually hot.

"Eddy, go outside, the house is on fire," his father said before he turned to me. "You get the young ones up, and I'll get Jer."

I wasn't afraid. I wasn't anything that can be described. I just went along as if it were perfectly natural, and I was calling everyone to get up for school. Eddy was ahead of me, opened Jer's door on the other side of the landing at the bottom of the stairs, and went inside, closing the door behind him. I quickly took the stairs two by two, and at the top I poked my head into Ida and Sharon's room.

"Get up! Get up!" I shouted. "You have to get out of the house." I noticed a haze in their room, but I thought it was my glasses steaming over from the heat. I didn't reach to check if I even had them on or not. I stood at the head of the stairs. "Francis, Neil, get up. Everyone get up. The house is on fire." Francis and Neil being the two oldest in each room on the front of the house, I figured they'd rally the rest.

The air moved as the door opened downstairs. Within seconds, smoke started to swirl around me. I shouted again and louder, "Get up! Get up! Come over here to me."

I believed they'd all hear me. I thought I heard sounds of them rising. Sharon and Ida were moving in the room next to me. I could make them out in the haze. I went back into my room and whipped the quilt off the bed. I grabbed the top sheet and twisted it around to make a rope. I ripped the bottom sheet from the mattress and wound that, too, and tied them both together. I tried the knot by pulling the sheets on either side of it to make sure it was secure.

I am sure I heard Barry say, "I can't see. I can't see."

I expected the young ones should have been right behind me by now. I turned and saw the room door had shut almost closed. I hadn't thought to push the small rock, used for that purpose, in front of it to keep it open. I grabbed the doorknob, and it was now hot to touch. I pulled it open and was met by smoke and flame. I tried to push forward, but the thick smoke billowed in quickly and choked me. Flames roared up the stairs. Everything was on fire: the floor, the walls, the ceiling.

I shouted for the children once more, but the noise was too loud and I gasped for breath, coughing between each word. Motherly instincts trampled on the natural instinct to run. The window behind me was the only escape. I thought that if I could get outside to fetch Eddy, we could get to the windows upstairs with a ladder. I knew I didn't have much time.

The flames gorged on the door frame as I struck at the windowpane with some force. The pane shattered, and a piece of glass sliced deep in my arm between my wrist and my elbow. A wide flap of flesh opened as I pulled back to clear the glass. Strangely, there was no blood. The bedsheet ropes were forgotten. There was no time to retrieve them, as the bed was now on fire. I hit the pane on the top section of the slider window. I needed a place to grab so I could lower myself down.

I sat on the sill and squeezed my body through the opening. It was about fifteen feet to the rocks below. I managed to get my legs out. I grabbed the sill as I turned myself to drop. I screamed out as I let go, and my fingertips grazed every clapboard on the way down. I crumpled in the ditch between the oil tank and the wall. I pushed myself up and raced around to the front of the house to get Eddy. I had no idea at this time where anyone was nor who needed rescuing.

As I rounded the corner, I met a crowd pulling Jer away toward the fence as sparks rained down on them. People were there, but I didn't see faces. Everything was out of focus. I searched the scampering crowd for the familiarity of Eddy, his face, his clothing, his movements, but couldn't see him. I noticed Neil and Larry first. I scanned for the others. I took a step. My bare feet were scraping on the rocks, but I didn't feel that.

"Where's Eddy?" I screamed. I needed him to check the windows upstairs. I needed to find the others. I took another step. I felt air whoosh by, and then I heard what sounded like a rubber sack of water hit the ground in front of me. I looked down.

To my astonishment, I realized it was Ida. "My God, she's dead," popped into my head and left my lips in a gasp.

I stooped beside her. I heard myself scream, "She's dead. She's dead," but again, I don't know where the words came from. I reached out to be sure it was her. Her body, blackened from smoke, was lifeless. Before I could touch her, she jumped up and ran off to the lower part of the meadow. I caught a glimpse of her rolling in the dewy grass.

I stood at the same time as Eddy came up behind me. He had the ladder in his hand, and he threw it toward the fence. By this time, cars and trucks arrived from all over the harbour, and people were coming into sight on the road in the distance. The house, immediately to my right and just a little out of reach, was burning. The heat was tremendous. People formed a line handing buckets of water, filled from the ocean, to each other right there in front of me. I was nailed fast to the ground.

There was noise, voices, honking horns, shouts, screams, heat, and the roar of the burning house. Somebody grabbed me and manoeuvred me toward a car. Somebody else had Ida. I can't say who it was, but we were brought to the shop.

Jos cried when she saw me. She had no idea what had happened, but there was chaos there, too. People talked and shouted over each other in the house as her children got up. There was crying and screaming and questions. I was like a robot by now. There was a ringing in my ears. All I could hear was noise. Jos said something about getting Ida to Placentia to the hospital. There was a sense of urgency around everything, but it didn't pass to me. Things were in slow motion. She wrapped my arm in a towel and pushed it toward my chest. I kept it there. I was naked but for the thin cotton nightdress and underwear I went to bed with on.

Jos threw a sheet over me. We were in the porch, though I didn't remember moving there. Jos tapped my leg. "Catherine, lift your leg till I get a pair of sneakers for you."

Hers were too small for me, so she grabbed Jud's and hauled them on over my feet. They were much too big, but she wouldn't let me go without something on my feet.

Seb's double-cab blue Chev pickup was outside and running. Jos helped us out of the house and down over the front steps. She wanted Ida to take a blanket and put something on her feet, but she refused. She wouldn't wear anything. Her bra and underpants were all she had on. She looked odd. Her skin was black.

I didn't protest being moved and guided. Seb opened the door to the front seat, and I got in. The rear doors opened and shut, Seb got behind the wheel. Then we left.

As we crested the small rise in the road, I saw the house. Thick black smoke billowed skyward. As we passed the graveyard and drew nearer, I saw the skeleton glowing yellow and red, and the beams collapsed on the outer corner. Plumes of smoke, ash, and sparks exploded. People moved back away from it.

So many people, so much pandemonium. Seb stopped and shouted for Eddy. He got in beside me, and I shoved in closer to Seb. You wouldn't know but we were going to a concert or a dance. Nothing seemed real. Eddy put his arm over my shoulders.

Seb and Eddy talked about what happened. They tried to figure out who saw who as they conversed back and forth over me. My arm throbbed. That was what I felt, besides numb.

"I saw Larry and Eddy," Eddy said.

"I think I saw Richard," Neil said from the back seat. "But I saw Larry and Eddy."

"What about Francis?" Eddy asked.

"I didn't see him," Neil said.

"Where's Larry?" I asked, suddenly afraid he'd have a seizure, and nobody would be there to help him.

"He was in the meadow near the woodpile," Eddy said.

"He should have come with us. What if he gets sick?" My voice was not my own. I didn't recognize it.

"I'm sure somebody will look out for him," Eddy said.

Neil kept asking Ida if she was all right, and I didn't know why. I turned around to look at her a few times. She was sitting forward in the seat with her arms straight out from her shoulders and bent at the elbows. Her skin was covered in webs. I was confused as to where she would have gotten those, but I didn't ask. She was rocking back and forth on the seat.

Seb spared no time as he raced toward the hospital in Placentia. It normally took over an hour with the dirt roads, but he wasn't giving much care to the potholes. Several times the rear fishtailed as he hauled one way or another clear of a hole.

A moose came out on the road, and it wouldn't let us pass. Neil got out and threw rocks at it, and Seb honked the horn.

For a minute, it would not budge. Finally, Neil threw more rocks, and without care for our urgency, it sauntered off the road. Neil jumped back in, and Seb gave it a wide berth and another honk as he passed.

He pulled in at the hospital an eternity later. Eddy helped me out. He told Ida and Neil to stay in the truck. Seb went ahead of us up the ramp and pulled opened the massive metal door on the second floor of the Placentia Cottage Hospital, at the ambulatory clinic.

We met Dr. Penney in the hallway. "Marg called," he said as he guided us to a private room halfway down the hall.

He asked us a few questions that Eddy answered. We sat in the room for hours. People called to see how we were doing. Every now and again, somebody would peep in at us from the corridor. Dr. Penney came and stitched my arm.

Larry had indeed had a seizure, according to Dr. Penney. Mike Tremblett had brought him in, though I didn't see him. Dr. Penney told me I had to stay for the night. Father McGettigan came to see me and said some prayers.

I couldn't get my mother and father off my mind. My cousin Marion Maher came to see me later that morning.

"I'm going out, Catherine. Can I get you anything?"

"Can you go see Mom and my father, see how they're doing?"

"I'll do that," she said.

Eddy went with her. She returned later that evening with clothes for me. A top and slacks, socks, shoes, and underwear she'd bought at the mall.

"Your mother is all right, despite it all," she said.

I was relieved.

"The doctor said you'll get out tomorrow. I'll bring you home."

I stayed all night, not leaving that room until the next day. I don't know if I slept or if I was awake all night. All I remembered was staring at the wall. My arm was bandaged, I took pills for pain, but I felt none. Strangely, I didn't feel anything.

Going out Placentia Road and down into North Harbour, the familiar was comforting. I was going home, and this would all be over. When we got to Kenneth's Hill, that's where familiar ended, and any reassurance that things would ever be normal again left with a mighty kick to the stomach.

The house still lay smouldering, a thin ghostly veil of smoke strung across the road, and the acrid smell of tar and wood and something indescribable lay in the air. There were police cars and other vehicles lining the road and the yard. We passed the scene, and Marion brought me to my parents' house.

Mom, making no effort otherwise, cried when she saw me. She hugged me and sobbed until she couldn't stand. Marg rushed in from next door. Mary was there, and Larry, too. The two Eddys and Neil were up in the meadow. I didn't see Ida. After the conversation going on in Seb's vehicle, I didn't ask about the others. Instinct or motherhood, or perhaps both, told me they were gone. I didn't comprehend what that meant.

"Where's Ida?" I looked around the room expecting her to bolt from somewhere.

"She's in the hospital," Marg said.

"I didn't see her. Dr. Penney didn't mention she was there. She could have come out with us."

"No," Marg said. "She's in the hospital in St. John's."

I whipped around. "What? What happened to her?"

She was burned," Marg said.

"Burned?"

"Yes," Marg said. Her raised brows and sullen frown moved up and down as she gently nodded.

I stared at her for a moment. "How could that be? She was all right when she came in with us."

"She wasn't, Catherine."

I searched my mind. I'd looked back at her in the truck. She was talking. I think she was. She was sitting awkwardly, arms out and bent, covered in webs. Then I realized what I had thought to be webs must have been skin. My legs gave way. I sat and put my head in my hands and jabbed my elbows into the table.

"How is she?" My question came through my fingers.

"We don't know yet. I'll call again when I go up home," Marg said. "I have the number up there."

Father Val Power and Sister Patricia Tobin came in. He'd been speaking with the investigators from the RCMP.

"They only have four," he said. "Is everyone sure that Francis was home?"

"He was home," I said. "I waited up until I heard the last of them come in. He was home."

"You're sure?"

"Yes, I'm sure." I was succinct in my answer. I was sure.

"Some swear they heard Richard was out, but nobody saw him. Did you see him?" Father Val pulled out the chair and moved in to the table.

"No," I said.

"You're sure?" Father Val asked as he reached over and patted my arm.

I nodded, my head still in my hands.

"Okay, I'll go back and tell them to keep looking."

Somebody laid a cup of tea in front of me. I drank it. I drank numerous cups that day. People came and went. The house was full, then empty, then full again. I stayed at the end of the table.

Father Val returned with news that they'd found who they assumed to be Barry. He was the smallest. They had trouble locating him. The youngsters would be brought to the morgue at the Health Sciences Centre. I knew I was supposed to be devastated. Perhaps I was.

I believe I was nothing.

13

Salt Fish

There's a place you go. It has no boundaries, no doors, no walls, but exists to catch you and pat you back together after you're scattered and strewn. I don't think anyone enters this place unwillingly. Though your feet have not moved, parts of you have journeyed.

This place exists for you to wait and adjust and repair. A place where you can take a little piece of information at a time and sit with it and dwell, make it real, come to terms with it, then take another little piece, and keep going until you've allowed it all in. Like the seconds on a clock. You don't tick into the next second until everything in your "dwelling second" is absorbed. Then tick, you go to the next second. Nobody knows you're there. It is not seen on your face or in your demeanour. It's private, internal, and your own.

Maybe you don't even know you're there in the beginning. You move, you speak, you do and say things that don't make sense or perhaps do make sense, you don't know. You are not where you body is. You are disconnected except for the few threads that keep pieces of yourself grounded though separated, waiting to become a new whole.

You do things that you think others expect. You may even laugh, you may even cry. It's your place. You stay there as long as you need it, days, months, years between each tick, until your dwelling place exists no more and you have been put back together changed.

Francis.

Tick.

Richard.

Tick.

Sharon.

Tick.

Harold.

Tick.

Barry.

Tick.

Then the worldly things. We had no money. That might be important.

Tick.

We had nothing. That might be important. Tick.

But the funerals had to be paid for. That was important.

Marg called Social Services for us and made arrangements to pay Dunphy's Funeral Home the cost. It would be almost $25,000 for a "base" package, so I was told. What that meant, I had no idea. But I agreed.

Tick.

Eddy hated owing anyone for anything. He wanted to pay for the funeral himself, but there was nothing we could do. We just didn't have the "it" required, and "it" was important. So, because that was troubling him, that trouble troubled me.

There were no savings rearing ten children. I'd never been inside a bank. It was one thing after another after another that took every cent we had. We had been clawing and crawling through the underbelly of poverty all our lives.

Now our belief was that we were indebted to the Welfare Office. We couldn't afford flowers, and I had no idea why a bloody flower mattered. It seemed appropriate, though.

The hours passed externally. I lost time. Maybe I went to that place to dwell and it swaddled me somewhere, I don't know. Before I knew anything again, I was in the church the next afternoon.

The caskets were brought in.

Five of them.

I had to say goodbye to a wooden box. Five . . . closed . . . wooden . . . boxes.

I couldn't touch my children, make sure they were all right, make sure they looked like themselves, kiss a forehead, stroke a cheek, set a pair—no, five pairs—of rosary beads between their fingers.

Nothing.

Worst of all, I couldn't make sure they were in there, that they were mine.

This didn't ever get a tick. I was stuck with not knowing. With doubt.

The small church was packed with people. Inside. Outside. A sea of faces. Sniffles, crying, and wailing all around me. Black suits and community members pushed the boxes to the altar. The wheels squeaked as the biers were rolled in. Even those were borrowed.

"Poor Francis," I said to nobody in particular as the first one came in. My voice and the squeak that bounced off the ceiling and the pillars and the altar before breaching loudly in my ears seemed like the only sounds now.

"Poor Richard."

"Poor Sharon."

"Poor Harold."

"Poor Barry."

They were all in and lined up at the face of the altar. There had never been the like here. I believe I may have cried because that is what I was supposed to, as a mother, do.

A line of people crushed to the front. Noise penetrated my core once again. Some cried openly, some tried to hold it back. I didn't know a soul. These were family, neighbours, and friends mixed in among strangers, but I couldn't put a name to a face.

I wanted to feel something. This shock and awe that stripped my emotions bare and left me raw had me fragmented and confused. I was disconnected from the gravity of what was transpiring. I didn't believe I was me. I couldn't tell you what a "me" would look like.

Perhaps if somebody told me what was happening, acknowledged that I'd lost my children, I would feel that pain of loss.

Those who could approach me spoke distant whispers of "sorry for your loss," or "sorry for your troubles." But nobody looked me in the eye, held my face between their palms, and said, "Catherine, your children are dead." Then, repeat this over and over until realization dawned in my eyes, in my heart. Maybe that would bring me from my stupor.

Did not feeling a desperate sadness, a devouring misery, mean it wasn't real? I didn't know. It felt like reality had disappeared and put this insanity in its place, that I'd wake up and things would be normal again.

For hours and hours, people came and went. Sounds of mourning filled the church, filled the harbour, and filled the bay. I was numb and lost. A part of me was enclosed and alone, and I didn't want to break free. Everything was moving, but nothing was moving while everything was moving.

It struck me that me and Eddy were supposed to go to my nephew's (May's son Cecil) ordination into the Christian Brothers the next day. It was a commitment I'd made and now couldn't do. I called him and told him to go ahead with what he had planned but that I was sorry that I couldn't make it. It was like things were just going ahead as normal, and things I was expected to do, I was still expected to do them. At least I thought I was. Or maybe I think I thought I was. I could chase that around in circles without finding the answer to what I was experiencing, but the dizzying effect was present.

Saturday went by. People came to the little church on the hill in the thousands. I sat in the front pew and stared at the red curtain behind the altar. I engaged with as few as possible.

In a way, I was afraid I wasn't enough of something, but I didn't know what that something was. I felt every eye bore into me and judge me on how sad I was compared to how sad I should be. But how would anyone know what that was supposed to look like?

The youngsters' friends came, the teachers at Our Lady of Mount Carmel, clergy, and strangers. I'm sure people sat for hours, conversations happened, but there was no celebration of the lives lost like might happen for the aged. No stories of "remember the time" or tributes to a life well-lived. It didn't fit. It wasn't supposed to.

"Catherine, is there anything I can do for you?" my cousin Imelda asked as she clasped my hand and brought me into the present. I thought about it, intending to say no.

"I'll tell you now, if I had a feed of salt fish, I think I'd be all right." Mom swore salt fish or salt herring would cure anything. Any time she was sick with migraines or a flu, she often wished for some kind of salt fish to make her better. That was it. That was what might work for me and take me out of whatever *this* was.

"Well, you'll have it tomorrow," she said. She didn't blink nor think it odd. She knew how much Mom, her aunt, swore by the cure.

Tomorrow was the burial. "That would be nice," I said flatly. I meant it. It would be nice to be better for the funeral.

The next day, somebody had sent down bags of clothes to Mom's for us to pick through. I got something to fit and pulled it on. So did Eddy. Somebody else stopped there to pick us up and bring us to the church. Nobody had a name or a face that I could recognize. I merely nodded and went along beside Eddy.

After spending a few hours at the church, Eddy and I left to walk to Imelda's, which was five minutes away. Preparations were being made at the church, and I guess that's why Imelda wanted us out of there at that exact time. No doubt Marg had had some kind of hand in it as well.

The plates were steaming when she laid them on the table. We ate salt fish and potatoes, me out of hope more than out of hunger. Imelda was a good cook and took pride in what she did. She was trying her best to make us as physically comfortable as possible. We talked about the weather, the crowds, and other unimportant things. The meal was very good. It was after 12:30 p.m. when we finished.

"Thanks for the fish," I said. "I can do the dishes."

"You will not," she scolded. "You have enough to be at today."

We got ready to leave when she assured me she'd take care of the dishes later. I was going out the door when I noticed the box of tissues on the table by the phone. I went back in and grabbed a bunch. "I guess I might need these," I said as nonchalantly as if it was an everyday occurrence I was going to. We left as I stuffed some in my pocket. We walked back to the church in silence.

Eddy had been stumbling around since the evening before. He complained he was off-balance and his ear pained. He had lost his glasses in the fire after leaving them on the little table by the bed. He couldn't get a good prescription for them on short notice. Besides, he had no money to pay for them, either. The lack of a good prescription could be another reason he was stumbling. We didn't know.

It came back to me that we had gone in to the Veterans Affairs Office in St. John's on Friday morning before the coffins were brought out. Marg accompanied us. Eddy asked them to help with glasses and the funeral costs, but there was no program for that, they said. They offered him a box of glasses from a new recycling program. He picked through them until he found the strongest pair. They still didn't work for him but were better than nothing until he got an eye appointment and new ones.

I was mortified that people would think he was drunk. Our outward appearance was important. I acknowledged that at least mortified was an emotion.

Marg, our anchor in it all, planned the arrangements for Mass with Father Val and Dunphy's Funeral Home despite the deficit of funds. The unexpected numbers of people were overwhelming, and there was no way the church would fit even a tiny fraction of the crowd. The plan was made to have the burial Mass on Lucy Fogarty's meadow. At the top of the big open field was a huge rock that would do for the altar. The meadow could hold 1,000 people, so it should have been fine.

However, cars began arriving hours before the 2:00 p.m. Mass of Christian burial. Because it was a Catholic Mass, the actual funeral Mass could not be said on Sunday. So, there would be two. In keeping with the regulations, the burial would be on the third day after the death, Sunday, and the funeral Mass would be the next day. Bishop Penney was coming with an entourage of other clergy for the burial.

I learned later that cars lined both sides of the dirt road for over two miles in each direction from the church and meadow. Some people walked for up to an hour to make it for the service.

Walking back into the church, I came to a realization. Salt fish didn't cure everything.

14

The Trials of Time

I think time went on in some horrendous way without me. I was swept up in the actions of the rest of that day, but my mind was back on Wednesday night when I sprinkled the holy water and went to bed. I relived that night over and over. What could I have done differently? How could I have gotten them out? There was a fervent and now a frantic hope I could go back and do something, anything, different.

My children were gone, and I should go on this path kicking and screaming and pushing my shoulder against time to go back to the day before the fire or to leave this dream. But I didn't know how. I didn't know how to go forward, either. I know I didn't want to, that was for sure. Each second that ticked, and the more I absorbed, the way back got farther from the last time they were all here. Fixing this was insurmountable, and insurmountable was piling up.

The darkest time of my being was upon me, and I didn't know how to act or what to say. I was caught inside my mind trying to change things. I fell to the rote of tradition and ceremony to get me through the coming minutes. Nature alone was cause for my breathing. Every single bit of me wanted to be with Francis, Richard, Sharon, Harold, and Barry. They were on a journey I didn't know. They were without me, alone and probably scared.

Nor did I know whether I should be there with them instead of here. How would I know where I was needed most? Did I take the fact that I was spared to mean that this is what was meant to be? How could I accept that? How could I learn to accept that?

I plotted against time, against circumstance, against everything that was happening, on how to go back. There must be something. It couldn't be real. It had to be righted before they were committed to the ground.

Wheels squeaked on the carriers as the children were readied to move. I wanted to scream "STOP" so I could find the answer. I remained silent.

I wanted somebody to prove they were in the caskets. I needed somebody to pull off the lids and show me their faces. I needed my tears to go with them.

I stared at nothing, a place between what was real and what I wanted to be real, as the senior Mr. Dunphy directed the order of exit. People lined up on either side of each coffin. White gloves clasped the handles and moved down the aisle. Dunphy beckoned for us to leave the seat. I believe I was crying out to them as they were being pushed away from us. Loud cries came from all corners of the church. Grown men had tears. Eddy was firm and strong by my side. He didn't buckle under the load. I wouldn't, either. I wouldn't, for their sake and not for my own.

There was ordered chaos outside as the coffins were manoeuvred to go down the ramp and crowds tripped in each other to move back. Then the pallbearers turned at the bottom of the ramp to walk to the meadow. The crowd parted, then closed in like they were water, and we were a ship upon the sea. I didn't feel buoyed, though.

I was drowning.

We paraded from the church, down through the graveyard, and then after a few minutes on the road, we reached the grassy field. A line of coffins carried by family, teachers, and friends was ahead of us, and whoever was at the church or in the yard were all around us. The crowd, already filling the field, opened and closed to swallow us as we made our way toward the rock at the top of the hill. I thought it was the longest walk of my life. I was breathless. I wanted to die.

A multitude of robed men commenced the Mass, and I stared. I believe I may have cried because I was supposed to, but I can't be certain. My mind left me for a while. I was afraid Larry was going to have a seizure, Eddy was going to be blamed for being drunk, and Little Eddy was going to hit the bishop.

I could picture Little Eddy walking up to Bishop Penney and walloping him right in the face. I tried to position myself to stop the assault. I focused on that because that made sense to me. It seemed so far-fetched to be a reality, but then look at what I was dealing with. It was easier to defend the bishop.

Faces swarmed and blended until all I saw was a blur of greys on a grey palette. Words were formed and spoken, though I couldn't tell you to this day what they were or who said them. I would have heard them before, though. There would have been prayers said that were part of the Mass I'd recited my whole life. That much I knew.

Prayers finished, and the parade returned to the graveyard. I thought coming to Lucy Fogarty's meadow was the longest walk of my life. I was wrong.

People were picking through the rubble of the burned-out remains of the house. The day turned sunny but not too sunny. People were sitting on the tailgate of a pickup truck. I was burying five children. Thoughts were just scattered with no sense of reason or togetherness. Everything was disjointed.

When we got to the road, I noticed Mary. She was ahead of us, crying and walking alone, her head down as she went. I wanted somebody to see that she was there. I should tell somebody to go to her. I looked around to get somebody's attention. But before I could, Ken Dunphy, the undertaker's son, ran up to her and linked into her arm. He had tissues and escorted her to the graveyard. That worry left me.

At the hole in the ground, the coffins were readied to be lowered.

"Poor Francis."

"Poor Richard."

"Poor Sharon."

"Poor Harold."

"Poor Barry."

Eddy had his arms around my shoulders. My eyes were searching for Larry and Little Eddy. I was still expecting Larry to fall and the bishop to be in mortal danger. I had to be prepared. Nurse and peacekeeper were my roles in that moment. I didn't want to be the grieving mother. That was just too much to ask of myself.

Holy water was sprinkled and prayers said once again. There was a deep silence broken only by the sound of the ropes stretching and groaning at the weight they bore. I'm sure there was crying, but the rope sounds were deafening. Eddy pushed away from me once the caskets were all out of sight. He moved to the black void that had my children and asked for a hand down.

"They're not right," he insisted. He moved from one box to the other to try and line them with the "head" of the grave. The boxes had been turned around and were resting at what he figured was the foot of the grave. After the few gasps at the extraordinary scene, and when people understood what he was doing, a few men got down in the hole with him and helped move the coffins. Nobody dared question what he wanted. They just followed his lead while everyone else stared open-mouthed from above.

Once he had them fixed to his liking, somebody reached out a hand and helped pull him and the others out. The crowd's mouths closed. Eddy stumbled toward me and almost fell when he grabbed my arm.

I was mortified again. People would really believe he was drunk. We'd never live this down. I was mad with him, another emotion. I was still looking for Larry. I was watching the bishop in case Little Eddy went after him. These thoughts kept circling faster and faster so nothing else could get in between reality and the cyclone.

After that, we all lined up again on the fake green grassy carpet that covered the edge of the opening. Prayers were said, and the bishop picked up a handful of clay. He reached out over the grave and let it slip through his fingers while he spoke. The hollow boom of each particle as it struck the boxes reverberated through my soul. More prayers finished the ceremony, and then we blessed ourselves.

People dispersed. Their eyes focused downward as they passed us by. Crying faded. Eddy grabbed my arm and pulled me away behind the crowd. We walked to my parents' house in silence. The last few days were clear yet were a fog. The world-turned-upside-downness of it all was too much to grasp in those few days. Maybe tomorrow would be better.

A lot of somebodies estimated that there were about 5,000 people in attendance. Somebody else thought it was a good day to bring up the issue of the potholes in the dirt road. Me, I watched time pass in bursts and stops since Thursday morning and wondered how I'd gotten to Sunday.

Later that evening, Eddy became disoriented to the point he couldn't stand up. He went to the Placentia Cottage Hospital for the second time since Thursday. He had a severe ear infection, and they kept him in.

At the funeral Mass the next day, I stood alone in a packed church. Internal panic beset me. Time kept racing away from the thing that I needed to fix, the nightmare I needed to awaken from, the catastrophe that needed resetting. The farther away I got, the less chance I had of making it right. For some reason, I thought the power was in me to somehow make it right. I was mad that I couldn't figure it out and that it might, inevitably, be too late. I couldn't accept that "too late" had happened almost four days before.

When Mass was over, a blur of people melded into one faceless image, a sea of voices turned into a foreign language, and I helped myself along from pew to pew as I followed an age-old mourning train to the door. I went to the black square of muddied earth with the five white Crosses lining its edge. I closed my eyes and hoped to awaken from the nightmare. I begged a prayer of undoing that was akin to asking the sun to rise in the west. I opened my eyes and grimaced at the unchanged scene confronting me.

The grass, trampled around the graves the day before, was springing back as nature intended. The birds sang, the bees buzzed, the flies paid no attention to my suffering nor to my discord with how things were naturally supposed to be— mothers didn't outlive their children. I swallowed the cauldron that bubbled and burned in my throat, then turned and went back to Mom's.

I had to find out about Eddy in the hospital in Placentia and about Ida in the hospital in St. John's.

I struggled to hold myself together so I would be able to hold fast to what was left.

15

A Much Different Normal

I stepped off the elevator. My hands were shaking, and I had difficulty focusing on the numbers emblazoned white against a light blue background. An arrow pointed to the right for Four South A with a range of room numbers that I didn't take notice of. I was like a mouse in a maze, moving past corridors with numbers that didn't match the one that Ida was in.

After going the wrong way several times, I passed another set of elevators, and the sign pointed left this time for 4-272 to 4-276. I rounded the bank of elevators and was confronted by a set of double doors that had a big red stop sign that I couldn't miss. Paper, stuck on with loops of Scotch tape, blocked the view on the inside of the mesh-lined glass. Another sign said RING FOR ACCESS and pointed to a button near the door casing. The locked barrier prevented not only physical but observational access.

I backed up and rechecked the sign to be sure this was where 4-272 and Ida were. It was. She was locked away. Three orangey-red couches were positioned in front of a large window that overlooked the roof of the second floor and the parking lot. My legs were shaky, so I sat for a few moments to compose myself.

I thought somebody might come through the doors and say "Ida who?" when I'd ask. They'd tell me there was no such person at the hospital, and I'd go home and wake up to relive the day before June 19 and wake up the next morning to the first day of summer holidays for the children and only have Larry to get ready for the bus so he could go to finish his exams. I stared through the window, then glanced at the door. No matter how hard I looked and how much I silently pleaded with it to open, it didn't. I only had an hour until Seb was going to pick me up. I pushed myself from the couch and moved to the doors. I pressed the button, I closed my eyes, I stopped breathing as my heart pounded in my ears, and a buzzing noise seeped through the door from where Ida was.

The door clicked, and I felt the air push past my face before I opened my eyes. A woman with smiling eyes between a paper cap and mask greeted me.

"Is Ida here?" I blurted out.

"Who are you?" the woman asked.

"Catherine, her mother."

"Mrs. Linehan?"

"Yes, Catherine Linehan. I'm Ida's mother. Is she here?"

"Come in. I'm Rusty. Ida's here." She pointed to a room just inside the door. I made a step to go where she had pointed, but Rusty's hand, gentle yet firm on my arm, stopped me.

"I'm sorry, Mrs. Linehan. You can't go in there."

"Why can't I?"

"Well, you can't go in there like that," she said as she gestured toward my clothing. "Ida is in a very fragile state. You need to have your garb on before you go in. Come over here until I get you ready."

"How is she?" I asked as Rusty guided me to a chair. "You must prepare yourself, Mrs. Linehan. Ida is not like you remember her." That brought me back to when I last saw her in the back of Seb's truck. I thought there were webs hanging off of her. I nodded. I believed I knew what she meant.

Rusty helped me put booties over my shoes, she gave me a hat and mask, and gestured for me to put them on. She held up a yellow hospital gown for me to shove my arms through. She tied it behind my neck and back. Then she gave me latex gloves to cover my hands. She chattered reassuringly while she worked to prepare me for the visit, but all I heard was a garbled and distorted voice as my eyes fixed on the room.

She pushed back the door and waved me in. "She can hear you. Talk normally. She had morphine just before you came, so she may be a bit groggy."

The room was small but somehow an arena at the same time. I took a few steps toward the bed in the dim light filtering through the mostly closed drapes.

What I saw wasn't Ida. I turned back to tell Rusty she had sent me to the wrong room, but the heavy wooden door was closing as she left. I turned back toward the bed. A large paper sheet covered whoever was there. The slight rise and fall of the stiff white material beckoned me onward. I moved slowly with my neck craned to see who was there and ready to bolt when I could say for certain it wasn't Ida. I grabbed the rail at the foot of the bed and used it to reel myself to the top. Hand over hand I moved, each step was getting harder with my body sinking and at war with my need to see who this was.

IV lines dripped—not just one, but several—and disappeared somewhere beneath the sheet at the bottom of the bed. Machines scribbled pointed lines on graph paper. Numbers blinked neon blue, and a beep rhythmically mirrored each step that I took.

I closed my eyes, afraid to look. I stopped where the rail ended. I slowly opened my eyes and gazed down at the figure in the bed. She was covered in bandages and was swollen almost beyond recognition. But from what little I could see around her eyes, I knew it was Ida. She didn't look at me. She was staring unseeing at the ceiling.

"I'm sorry," I whispered. "I'm sorry." I reached out to touch something, somewhere, on her that was safe. But there was nowhere. Tears sprang forth, and I left the room. In my heart, I knew there would be another child in the graveyard within a few days. I never in my wildest thoughts had imagined that she was as bad as this.

I expected Ida to be sat up in the bed, or on a chair, eager to see me. She'd be waiting for me to come in and take her home. I was trying to figure out how to tell her all that happened, but that wouldn't be necessary now. She was dying. I was not prepared for this. For any of this.

Out by the door, I asked Rusty what had happened. I explained about the last time I saw her.

"She doesn't look like my Ida," I stammered. "You're sure it's her?"

"There's nobody else here on the burn unit," Rusty said, her eyes crinkling as she smiled beneath the mask.

"I just can't believe it's her."

"That's all the fluids we're pouring into her. She needs to be hydrated. But her kidneys are not working, either, so everything is going in, but nothing is coming out."

"All the bandages. Is she in pain?"

"We're keeping her comfortable."

"Will she live?"

"I'd like to think she will. It's going to be a long road for her, though. But I've seen others burned like this and worse who have survived. I won't lie to you, Mrs. Linehan," Rusty said. "I can't tell you that she will live, either. The doctor is on his way up."

"I can't stay here when they're doing anything with her. I have to go."

I regretted having left so quickly. I didn't get to tell Ida that I loved her. She knew. I was sure of that. I sat silently in the back seat of Seb's truck and closed my eyes. I couldn't allow myself to weep. I knew if I cried I'd fill the ocean. I prayed there was some way this was a nightmare and I'd soon wake up. Maybe I was dead myself and gone to hell. Perhaps that was the way of it.

The next week, Seb was going to St. John's and called to see if I wanted to go back to see Ida. Marg had called every day, and whoever was on duty said she was doing well. They called me the day after I left, asking for consent to operate on Ida because of her kidneys. I gave it over the phone. Marg called that evening and was told that Ida's kidneys had begun to function on their own and she was doing much better.

This time, I remembered the way to the room, and I rang the bell. Rusty was there again and helped me get outfitted for my visit. "She's doing much better, Mrs. Linehan. It may not look like it, but I am telling you, she will be just fine. It will take a long time, but she'll be just fine."

This time, the room light was on and the drapes were pushed back. There was a regular white sheet on the bed today and not the paper one from the week before. Rusty told me she hadn't had anything to eat or drink yet and showed me how to swish a sponge stick around in her mouth to keep it from drying out.

She did it for me, and Ida's lips moved, and she muttered something that whispered hoarsely like a thank you.

I talked to her and told her I was there. She moved her head toward my voice. Her arms were covered from the shoulders to the fingertips with bandages, others covered her chest and neck, and patches of square bandages stretched across cheeks and nose. Her hair was short, broken, and blistered at the tips where it had been scorched in the flames. I would not allow myself to close my eyes to block out the image. I knew she was suffering. I kept looking at her and smiling and suffered right along with her.

Rusty came in and asked me to go out and sign papers allowing the hospital to care for Ida. That would save them having to call each time Ida needed a procedure.

"She's going to the operating room today," Rusty said.

"Today?"

"Yes, we were about to call you when you came in."

She explained why the doctors were operating, but I didn't want to listen. I couldn't bear to hear anything about what they were doing. Ida would be hurting and in pain, and I couldn't take that from her to carry myself. I went back in her room for a few minutes before Rusty returned, and I prayed to God for her to make it.

"They're coming for her now," she said. "Ida, you're going into surgery." Two nurses followed Rusty, and two men in white uniforms pushed a gurney into the room.

The rail clicked, and panic set in. My heart went a mile a minute, and I got up and left. I didn't get the chance to tell her I loved her, but I knew she knew.

"Catherine," I heard through a fog. "Catherine, where are you going? Catherine. Stop."

Harold Fowler was chasing after me as I crossed the road toward the bus stop. I didn't realize I was outside until he caught up with me.

"Where are you going?"

"I'm catching the bus to the Avalon Mall to wait for Seb Walsh."

"You're going like that?"

I looked down as he nodded toward me and eye-scanned me from head to toe. I still had on the booties, gloves, mask, gown, and head covering. I don't know how he had recognized me.

"It's Ida. She's going into surgery."

He nodded and gently reached out and took my arm to guide me back inside. I stripped the hospital garb, and he took it from me.

"I'll drop it in a bin on my way to my appointment."

I nodded my thanks, and he was gone before I got to ask him how he was doing.

My head cleared a little. I met up with Seb. That day I rode home in the back seat wondering if Ida would be all right. By the time I got to Marg's that evening, word had come in that she was okay and resting comfortably.

When people from the community were going to St. John's, they called me to see if I wanted to go in. I didn't refuse and got to spend bits of time with her in the coming months. I didn't tell her anything about what had happened. We didn't talk about why she was there. We just got through each visit. Ida seemed positive and smiled every single time when I went in.

Eddy didn't go. He got on with things. He asked me to ask Ida where she wanted him to build the house.

"I can't think of living anywhere else," she told me. It was settled. That's all Eddy wanted to hear. He began the process of rebuilding in the same yard a few feet in front of where the old house had burned.

The next trip in, Ida told the nurse to tell me she needed some pyjama bottoms so she could get out in the chair. I stopped at the Avalon Mall, and Jos and Seb said they'd meet me at the hospital when they had their business done.

By the time I made the purchase at Sears and caught a taxi to the hospital, more than an hour had passed. When I arrived, Jos and Seb were on the couches. I rushed forward. "What are they doing with her now?" I asked as I raced around the couch to face them. But there was somebody else there. Ida was sitting on the couch. "How?"

"Only for a few moments," Rusty said from the open door. "She wanted to surprise you."

I burst into tears, and I couldn't stop them. Though I'd practised holding them back for this milestone, the unexpectedness of it caught me off-guard. I reached out, then pulled back my hands. I couldn't hug her. I couldn't do anything except collapse into the chair and push back the traitorous tears.

I had to be strong for Ida.

Rusty and another nurse helped Ida up from the couch and guided her back to her room. She was unsteady on her feet and was tired after taking the twenty steps or so between the waiting area and her bed. She winced and groaned as the nurses put her back in the bed and fixed her arms on the cushions to keep them elevated.

"You can't do that again. You're not ready. But I'm proud of you," Rusty said as she put the finishing touches on Ida as if she were painting her. She looked toward me and grinned beneath the mask. "She's my girl, you know. She's special to me."

I nodded. I knew she was in good hands.

A few weeks later, I got mail from Ida. It was two pages with big, loopily handwritten letters telling me she had a lot of her bandages off and was learning to feed herself. She signed it, "All my love, Ida." Eddy was most proud of it. He held it for a long time before passing it back to me. I brought that letter with me to Marg's and to the store, where I showed it to anyone who would look at it. Everyone was excited that Ida was making such good progress.

16

Throw Out the New and Bring Back the Old

I glanced up from the yellow plastic pan where the two cups and plates lay waiting for water and a soapy cloth. The sound of the hammer had stopped. Eddy must be getting another board. He'd been at it today since daylight.

We didn't talk. Talking wouldn't change anything. We just went about what needed to be done. He was sealing the house, adding match lumber on the inside studs to make the house sturdier. I couldn't help but think that it would be more wood to burn.

The windows and doors would be here next week. A new house would be most people's dream. Not mine. I would have been glad enough to have the other one back, to have time reset, but I knew these were foolish thoughts. I had the same ones since it happened, and nothing changed. However, just having them was a comfort, because they brought possibility and miracles to mind.

Today I'd pass my forty-seventh birthday, cooking stew in the iron pot over an open fire by the gully that dissected the upper and lower meadows. The pot was one of the only things remaining from our former life, that and a ragged patch quilt that had been hanging on the fence overnight, as well as a brown glass mug with a wooden handle that sat on a trunk in the shed. It still held the dregs of Tang that either Ida or Sharon had left when they played table tennis there on the last rainy day.

When I glanced at the calendar at Mom's that morning and realized it was my birthday, I almost doubled over in pain. I recognized this was my first birthday. I was on this torturous and lonesome journey for eighty-nine days now. But today there was a knot on a thread that marked a milestone for me as being farther from what were now "before memories." I scowled at the thought of what "happy birthday" would be, because I had already had my last happy anything. The only thing that would suffice was my old life back, turning the clock to the eighteenth of June, and clearing this fog of unbelievability.

These were not new thoughts. They ran rampant upon my mind all the time now.

I stirred the fire, where I'd cooked every day for the last month or more. The kettle bottom reddened on the grate, and I poured boiling water on top of the Sunlight dish detergent I'd squirted in the corner. I dipped the pan in the river to add cold water and laid it on the bank nearest me. I threw a few dry sticks on the fire, refilled the kettle, and went about washing the plates, mugs, and utensils. I threw the dishwater on the bank downstream, rinsed the pan, and laid the dishes in.

After scrambling up the two-foot incline on the now worn pathway on the embankment, I grabbed the pan and carried it to the cut-out marked for the basement door. The MacDonalds from Mount Carmel would be over to lay the cement for the floor soon. But for now, the crushed stone skittered away from my feet as I walked to the small table near the centre of the house. Eddy was hammering again, and the echo inside the shell gave me a headache if I stayed there too long. I left quickly and crossed the small footbridge on the river on my way to the building that served on one end as a shed and the other end as a stable.

The step to the shed faced the house, and I remained there with my back to the ochre clapboard until Eddy came looking for tea. It was me and Eddy these days. Larry helped out where he could. But his father was afraid he'd have a seizure and fall from the upper floor, so Larry came and went as needed. Neil was working in St. John's. He'd work on the house the entire weekend, but weekdays, once he got home for the evening, he'd help his father until dark. Little Eddy had left for Alberta shortly after the funeral. I rarely heard from him.

I rubbed my bruised arm and rested it across my lap. A few days before, I'd climbed the two ladders to the main floor of the house. The place was designed to be a split entrance, so once I got off the first ladder that was anchored in the crushed stone, I grabbed the next one and started to climb. The entrance was only a platform at the time, no walls yet. When I reached the top of the second ladder, the bottom slipped on the plywood and slid out from under me. I grabbed for one of the studs that was in the upstairs wall just before the ladder gave way completely and disappeared in the rocks below.

I was using my bad arm that had been cut and was still numb to keep myself from falling. I tried to swing myself in toward another stud to hold on with two hands. There was nothing underneath me, but if I swung far enough, I'd fall on the landing instead of down into the basement if I missed the second stud.

Fortunately, Neil heard the crash and shouted to his father. The two of them grabbed me and pulled me up onto the main floor of the house. Eddy got such a fright, he got mad. Mad that I'd almost fallen, mad that I climbed up, mad that the ladder wasn't secure, and just simply mad. Neil jumped down and put the ladder back, this time driving a block into the plywood so that it wouldn't stir. When I got down, I swore I'd stay away from the house until my arm got better, as I was still miffed at Eddy for being mad.

Being stubborn, there I sat, almost a week later, waiting for the next time the kettle needed boiling. Emotions ran high in all of us now, maybe to crowd out the sadness.

All in all, our spirits had lifted a little bit now that Ida could come home. Though she went back the day before, it was nice to have something to look forward to on the weekend. Mary came out, too. Everyone had an underlying sadness, and there was nothing I could do about it. There was no fixing it.

For myself, I couldn't afford to be anything. I was afraid of emotion. I don't know if I couldn't cry or if I was steeling myself so I wouldn't cry. Though it was irrational, and I knew it, I feared that tears might wash away something about the youngsters and begin deconstructing or erasing the only thing I had left—memories.

Eddy came out the back door, and I went to work. We had the last cup of tea for the day on the riverbank. I washed the dishes once more, laid them away for the next day, and headed toward the graveyard. I stared unseeing at the patch of dark earth that sprouted grass and tried to blend with its surroundings. Except, of course, for the five Crosses. For a while I had been mad at the grass and plucked or stomped the blades when they poked above the ground. After the first hundred or so, I stopped the foolhardy errand.

Harold had already passed a birthday in August. I felt some shame in doing no more than touching the clay where he lay, and for a moment, a thought flashed through my mind as to if he had ever existed. But the red-headed little boy who claimed that homemade chocolate cake was his favourite was an image that was burning in my soul on what would have been his thirteenth birthday. That and the watery eyes of everyone whose startled gaze crossed mine and the constant ache in my heart reminded me that it was real, that they were all real.

But to torture myself a bit more, I found myself drifting into questioning if they existed after that. Not in a way that I didn't want them to have been, but from the sense that this couldn't have happened. The moments were fleeting but were moments just the same. Trying to align the two in my head was a constant churn. Then I'd admonish myself for such selfish and ungrateful thoughts. I couldn't think on how they must have suffered. That part left me weighing what was better, that they hadn't existed or that they had died horrifically.

It was impossible to reconcile what had happened almost three months ago with reality. I continued to what-if myself to death, and nothing changed. I swallowed hard, straightened my back, and walked away.

I darted to my mother's house. Both she and my father were a concern for me. They were trying too hard to be strong, especially Mom. I'm sure they were reliving Frank all over again. I heard her cry at night, though nobody cried in front of me. But I didn't cry, either.

Period.

I had my head down and watched the tiny rocks and gravel, disturbed by my boots, settle after each step. Some were kicked again with the next footfall. I was those rocks, the ones kicked again and again until they were somewhere they didn't recognize. It was easier to concentrate on such meaningless things than to think on my troubles.

But before I made it halfway up the lane to the house, Mom burst out the door.

"Catherine, Catherine, somebody is looking for Francis."

"What?"

"Somebody on the phone is looking for Francis. I can't understand what they're saying."

I went in ahead of her and picked up the phone from the chair in the hall. "Hello."

"Hello, ma'am, I'm calling for Francis Linehan. Can I speak to him, or can I leave a message with you for him?"

"Who's this?"

"Ma'am, is this the right number for Francis Linehan? The other number he gave us is out of service."

"I'm his mother. Who's this?"

"I'm calling from the provincial government. Francis applied for a job with our department several months ago. We have decided to hire him. Can you tell me how to get in touch with him?"

"I wish I could. Francis died in June." My words came out bluntly, in a tone bereft of feeling. A simple statement that said so much.

There was a long pause before the woman spoke on the other side of the line. "Oh, I am so sorry to hear that. I'm sorry for bothering you. We won't call again."

There was a click. I held the phone to my ear. Francis was gone. As I stared at the air somewhere between me and the wall, I hung up the phone using peripheral vision.

"Who was that?" my mother asked.

I told her it was somebody about a job.

Francis had left earlier in the spring to drive to Ontario for work. He got as far as the ferry in Port aux Basques and turned around and came home. If he had to keep going, he'd be alive now. So many "ifs" plagued my existence. Too many to count, but the ifs that pertained to me hurt the most. If I had only done this, or if I'd only done that. I shook my head and went to the kitchen.

Mom put on chicken for Larry. I told her me and Eddy would eat up at the house. I left and walked back up the road. I went to Marg's on the way along to tell her what happened. Marg had called the banks, the church, the school, the government, and anyone who needed calling to cancel accounts, get death certificates, to straighten out the records for all the youngsters. This was one thing she couldn't have foreseen. I don't know what I would have done without her.

Marg had kept strong in all of this. She had relieved so many burdens by taking what she could from me. I wouldn't have known where to begin. I was thankful for her.

Returning to our meadow, I heated the stew on the fire near the gully and waited for the others to arrive. One day dragged routinely, empty, into the other. Each morning that I woke to the once-familiar surroundings of my childhood at my parents' was one day farther from the familiarity of my children. It wasn't something I wanted to get used to doing, but I was getting used to it despite my mind's protest.

Everything hurt on the inside, even breathing, even knowing I was alive. People were speaking to me again. "Nice to see the sun" kind of talk, not, "Catherine, five of your children are gone" kind of talk. I was okay with that, though, I think. I wasn't sure how I'd be with the latter. But maybe it would quieten the space where I foolishly questioned their existence. How was I to know what would have helped? Or if anything helped?

Maybe in time.

Or so I'd heard. There would be some kind of peace in time. Maybe I'd said that a time or two when I didn't know the difference. There was no path I could follow where they didn't exist or I'd "get over" them. That was not possible. In the background, out of sight of the world, they remained beneath my skin. My silent tears and my closed heart ached because I knew them and loved them. Their absence would forever be present for me.

I had already frantically searched and excavated every morsel of a memory. I parsed them and sharpened their edges and pinned them to my mind so they wouldn't blend, fade, and erode into a generic "those were happy times" or "those were poor times" fashion often associated with youth. They had so many blank pages that they didn't get to write. I wanted a clear and firm grasp on those things they had experienced, we had experienced, so I could take them with me for as long as I could. I didn't know if there was a right way to go on. I now only knew the act of breathing and going through the motions of living. That was enough and all I could handle. I did what I had to do for those who still remained here and depended on me to be their mother, their wife, their daughter, their friend. I kept going for them. There was no self in anything I did.

"Why" remained unanswered no matter how many times I asked. How many times I will ask will depend on how many years I remain here without them. For the "now" of each day, I buried any thoughts of myself and moved forward. It wasn't a complaint or self-pity. It was how I forced myself to be alive without feeling like I was living.

I had to stop this questioning and believe what was before me. No matter how hard it would be was meant to be my suffering. The trouble was, my want to stop questioning and my will to believe didn't nor wouldn't align.

"Get out of bed" was the first of many a talking-to that I gave myself each day after that.

Part III

The After Compartment

_____

_____

17

New Roots in Old Dirt

It was October 31, 1980. We were moving into the new house and back on the land where we'd lost so much. Too much.

Home was no more. I knew that the moment I walked in that day. It was a house. Wood, bricks, nails, all part of a shelter. Warm without warmth, house without home, new without newness, in a complete world that would echo an incompleteness for as long as I lived.

Ida was still in St. John's, Neil and Larry were around but rarely seen, leaving me and Eddy by ourselves for the most part. Just a few months before, home was full, and now in this place we were staring at new walls, new ceilings, new everything. The dream of so many, but the nightmare for us. Stillness and silence were the most overwhelming.

With the house built, the dishes in the cupboard, and the beds made, there was another worry about what was going to take up time now. If I didn't have something to occupy my hands, I didn't know if my mind would survive.

Being Halloween, I bought candy at the shop and told Jos that we'd be in the house to give out treats. Something normal. She'd pass along the message.

My insides were wound tight the whole evening, but nobody came. Maybe that was a good thing. A blessing. I don't know how I would have thrown a bar or a drink in a bag when my own should have been at the doors and they weren't.

We turned off the lights at ten o'clock and went to bed. I didn't sleep that first night. "Ifs" were on replay from lie-down to the "get out of bed" sometime after dawn. It was easier that morning.

Once breakfast was cleared away the next day, Eddy went out at the wood. The clock ticked. I think I left it there instead of pelting it out in the beach so that it, too, would torture me. The echo of axe to stick was rhythmic. The clock was relentless in its pursuit of moving on.

I had to get out. I went to Marg's, and to Mom's, and to the graves. Another adjustment and a tightening of my composure was required.

Ida was having a hard time in school in St. John's, so I called Father Power to see what we could do. A new school principal, Sister Anne Campbell, had come to Our Lady of Mount Carmel, and I didn't know her. Father Power put me in touch with Sister Anne, and he explained the situation. Ida was in the hospital most mornings and found it difficult to participate in her grade eleven studies in such a large and strange environment for her, especially not being able to do it full-time. The new principal was understanding of my plight and told me to leave it with her.

I got a call an hour later, and Sister Anne told me that Ida didn't have to go to school in St. John's. She said that the teachers would ensure she had what she needed in the second half of the school year so that she could graduate. If she didn't get released from the daily trek to the hospital, she could do her final year the next year.

When I called Ida to tell her, there was a whoop on the other end of the phone. She assured me she'd work hard when she got back to Our Lady of Mount Carmel and graduate with her friends. I had no doubt she would.

By the end of November, she was home more frequently and was able to go to school on the bus for a day. I saw the life come back in her eyes. She was so weak but in many ways so strong.

December came, and I swore up and down that there would be no Christmas in the house. Ida kept coaxing me to put up a tree, but I was adamant. She told me she was going to do it anyway.

"Mom, if you don't have Christmas this year, you'll never have Christmas. We'll never have Christmas," Ida implored.

"I don't care about Christmas. We're not having it, and that's that." I didn't want anything celebrated. It wasn't right.

"Mom, Christmas will come whether you want to have it or not. It will be here."

"Not in this house," I said.

"I'm in this house, too," Ida said. "Things are sad enough. We don't need to make them worse."

"Having Christmas won't change anything." I felt anger rise, and I didn't want to be mad with Ida. She'd been through enough.

"It will for me," she said. "If you don't have Christmas here, then I'll stay with Nanny and Grandfather. Even they have a few things up."

"You'll do no such a thing." I walked away from the table and leaned on the counter in the kitchen.

"Indeed I will. Or I'll go to Marg's. They'll have Christmas for their youngsters," Ida said quietly.

She was defiant. I had never seen her like this before. I put my hands on the counter and stretched to peer out the window.

"Mom, I'm not trying to be mean, but I want something, anything, to be just a little bit normal," she said.

Eddy was lying on the daybed. He sat up. I heard his feet hit the floor and the springs creak when he moved.

"Catherine, can't you let her have it?" he asked. Then he took his coat and went outside.

The fridge shuddered to a stop, leaving nothing but the clock to make a sound. I turned around and looked at Ida.

"Just a small tree. That's it. No decorations around the house. Nothing else." I heard the words and couldn't stop them. My voice didn't seem my own. The brace that held my insides together slipped for a second, and I swallowed the tremble at the back of my throat.

She jumped up and came to the counter and hugged me.

"I promise. Just a small one." She squeezed my arm and hugged me again, then ran out after her father. I turned to the counter and pinched the lip on the countertop as hard as I could until my hands went numb.

I didn't think I could handle Christmas.

A few days later, Larry, Neil, and Ida went into the woods and cut a tree. I watched through the bedroom window as they hauled it down the hill and into the shed. Eddy squared it off with the handsaw. None of them looked happy or excited. Not like in years before, when the place would be teeming with crayon-coloured paper streamers, things hanging from the ceilings and doors, tinsel sparkling everywhere.

Children.

Children noise.

Children laughter.

I closed my eyes against the emptiness and prayed for the strength to keep going. I debated whether I would ban the tree to the downstairs and just not go down there. But then, I wouldn't do that. We all needed to work it out somehow.

The next day, the tree scraped along the railing and the wall as Larry and Neil carted it in. They had a white beef bucket of rocks to serve as a stand.

In the kitchen, I took the cards and played Queens with Eddy so I wouldn't have to go in the living room. Once the tree was up, Ida realized there were no ornaments. Not a thing. She left for the shop. Larry followed shortly after. They came back half an hour later with an armload of stuff.

I tuned out the sounds, dealt the cards when it was my turn, kept the score, and didn't say a word. Then Eddy asked me if we were having a lunch or not. I didn't realize how late it had gotten. I boiled the kettle, and we had tea and toast and jam. After I cleaned away, we went back to playing Queens once again.

Around three, I finished the card game and concentrated on supper. The noise from the soft rustles in the living room had quieted.

Catherine and Thomas Dalton came over nearly every evening around seven. There wasn't much said, normally. They had lost their daughter, Jackie, just months before the fire. She was the age of Francis. We shared a common torment in many respects. Them that goes through it are them that knows. I guessed that's why they came so often now. We sat out around the table that night.

It would be a few days before I ventured into the living room. I waited until I was alone the first time. I prepared myself. There were times things pushed on my thoughts. They were so confusing, I thought I was living another person's life. Going into the living room was one of those.

I watched myself go past the top of the stairs and take one step in the living room. I experienced it fractured. I was there, but I wasn't. I managed a glance first and left. I breathed in deeply by the table. I had trouble to catch my breath, and my chest pained.

I stared out the window and watched the still ocean. A few pecks of snow sauntered toward the ground. Without thinking about it, I turned quickly and scurried back into the living room. This time I got as far as the chesterfield. I sat for a moment. The back of my throat vibrated in its need to release what would choke me if I let free.

The tinsel was mesmerizing, drifting slightly as the air moved. The old bulbs that had adorned the tree for so many years were replaced by plain red, blue, and gold balls of string.

Balloons were missing. They used to be such a treat with the young ones scrubbing them across their hair and sticking them on the wall before shoving them in through the branches. Popping sounds and startled laughter.

Christmas cards would have lined the piece of twine that stretched across the corner holding the tree in place. There were none this year, coming in nor going out.

I sat with the tree. The silence wasn't as loud. I couldn't handle that it wasn't. I couldn't be comfortable. I got up and left.

That evening, I went in the living room and watched the news with the others. Nobody drew attention to my being there; we just watched television. My insides churned. Nobody noticed that, but maybe I didn't notice theirs, either.

My internal heart-rending reality and what I thought I displayed were out of sync, like I was living two lives. There was no doubt that an air of unspoken absence and grief emanated from me, making others wary of me. Not because they didn't care, but because they cared too much. So very few could handle meeting or speaking to "the woman that lost five children in the fire." It was hard enough for me to handle her. I didn't know how.

My private suffering and the constant replay of the events of June 19 were terribly isolating. I was alone on a rock in the middle of an ocean. I couldn't navigate the stormy seas.

Trying to control any outward grief was my daily grind, to both family and strangers alike. The time for grieving had passed, and it would be shocking to show any signs of sadness months after the tragedy. We were conditioned to the outwardness part of grieving being only borne publicly at the wake and funeral. It was now meant to be put behind me. But my mind and my heart couldn't agree on that precept. The constant struggle was a rabid madness on my soul. Adding Christmas to that? I didn't know what I was capable of bearing.

Mary came home for a few days from her work in St. John's. She brought a few gifts with her and placed them under the tree. She cried as she did that. I heard her sniffles through the walls but couldn't go to her.

Christmas Eve was upon me like a hungry cat on a mouse. It batted me, pushed me, hove me, and clove me as I opened my eyes that morning to the realization of the day.

The most recent years of Christmas Eves came rushing toward me. The pandemonium and fervour of the day was the best part. The youngsters couldn't wait for evening to come. The five youngest used to make two Kraft pizza box mixes. One was green and the other yellow. Part of the ritual was to go the store to get them that day. They'd bake them around six in the evening.

Big slabs of pizza and large glasses of cola would be laid out on chairs pulled close to the sofa. There wouldn't be a sound then as Christmas movies played on the television. There'd be chaos during commercials, then a shout of "it's on" and the rush to the seat they had vacated minutes before. The chairs would be put back to the table and the dishes carted out after the pizza was devoured. Then they'd go to bed. I shut my eyes on the memories, savouring what I could.

Last Christmas Eve, or what now was their last Christmas Eve, it was the first year that none of the youngsters believed.

It had been a little bit sad that that time was over. But Ida had asked me to do stockings, anyway, and to have Santa come. Unknowing of the desolation the next Christmas Eve would have brought, I'm glad that I had given in with very little resistance.

As the older ones got out working, they'd be so proud to pool their money to bring home things like a washer and dryer, a sofa, a fridge, or something "big" for me and their father for Christmas. Turkeys and hams were given out at work, with the biggest going to my boys because we had such a crowd at home.

Now I washed two mugs in the sink as me and Eddy finished up our breakfast. The day was going to be a torture.

But Marg and Dick came up before lunch. They stayed for a few hours. Not much was said, but Marg played cards with Eddy while Dick looked on. I knew they had lots of things to do, but Marg insisted they stay and have a bite to eat before going home.

With Neil, Larry, Ida, and Mary around the table, too, there was noise. I could breathe.

Shortly after Marg and Dick left, Jos and Seb came to visit. They stayed most of the afternoon engaging us in conversation.

Larry said he was going to get a pizza at the store and asked if I wanted anything. I shook my head. Tonight, I knew Larry would bring home the green box. That was his favourite.

When the dishes were cleared away after supper, Jos came back again. This time she had her teenaged son, Jud, with her. Jud was my godchild and in between Harold and Barry in age.

He was hesitant coming in behind his mother. She gave him a little push. He walked toward me with fear in his eyes and his arms outstretched, a small, wrapped gift in his hands.

I couldn't stop what happened next. I grabbed him and threw my arms around him and bawled. It took me a few minutes to force myself to stop, to close the release valve. I let him go and he backed up, red-faced. Poor young fellow, it was good of him to come. Jos was crying, too. They only stayed a short time.

Thomas and Catherine came over from the other side a little while later, staying a few hours. Not much was said, but it was a comforting and commiserating silence. Crossed legs swayed in unison to the sound of an old hockey game on in the living room. We got a lunch around eight o'clock before they left.

Larry made the pizza. Mary and Ida turned Christmas movies on. The mood was sombre when we all went to bed, but the day had whiled away a lot faster than I thought it would.

I slept fitfully though dreamlessly into Christmas Day. May and Cecil came over from St. Mary's without their kids and spent part of the day with us before returning home that evening. I went to see my mother and father before turning in for the night.

Christmas didn't kill me. The first one in this new reality was over.

New Year's Eve was never really a big deal at the house. Eddy and I sometimes went to a dance in Colinet to ring it in. Instead, we played cards. I didn't know if I should be glad it was over or if it was another knot in that thread that kept getting unmercifully longer every milestone.

But atop my mind were the thoughts of Neil and Larry leaving for Alberta in a few days. I was concerned for Larry most of all, but I said nothing. By January 3, they were gone. Mary went back to St. John's that Sunday, too. Ida was the only one home now. She'd start and finish her grade eleven in the next couple of months and by September would leave for college.

Nineteen eighty took most of my children from me, and it seemed like 1981 would, in a way, take the rest.

18

Where Once They Stood

Eddy, who was sixteen years my senior, retired from his job as river warden the next January and received his old-age pension. We didn't have a lot of money to get by on. The community had raised money to help us get into our house, and the last of it was used to purchase headstones.

Francis had worked with the Department of Transportation, and Marg found out that he had a small life insurance through them. She applied, and that spring a cheque for $25,000 came in Eddy's name. He was Francis's beneficiary. Eddy signed it. He took an envelope, poked it inside, and sent it to the Welfare Office in St. Mary's to cover the children's funeral expenses. He said that Francis would have wanted it that way.

It was just the two of us for the next couple of years. The children, now grown-ups, ebbed and flowed through the house. Ida had surgeries and needed care for weeks at a time. Those things gave solace of hands to take from the pain of the mind and the heart.

The first snowfall, the birthdays, and June 19, 1981, battered me and changed me to a point I almost didn't recognize myself. But sadly, those things wouldn't be the worst of it.

In May 1983, a police car pulled up in the driveway. A young officer got out and approached the door. I was petrified for the moment when I answered the knock. All kinds of thoughts raced through my mind; foremost was a plea that it wouldn't be news that something had happened to one of the remaining children.

My heart was pounding in my ears when he spoke.

"Are you Catherine Linehan?" he asked.

I nodded, mouth open, waiting for the collapsing news.

"I have a subpoena," he said as he handed me a paper.

My thoughts were swirling around, and I was confused. "What?"

"A subpoena to appear in court."

"Court?"

"June 24. Is your husband here?" his starched and polished persona asked.

"Yes, he's gone in the woods."

"I'll leave these with you, then," he said as he handed me several envelopes and then turned and left.

I backed into the porch and used the wall to support me. I rifled through the envelopes. My name, the two Eddys, Neil, Larry, and Ida. I staggered in as far as the table and flopped on the chair as the sound of the car engine fired and the tire sounds on the gravel faded.

I opened the envelope. Big bold letters faced me on the yellow paper.

Enquiry.

There was going to be an enquiry at the courthouse in Placentia.

Fear, anger, and confusion raced each other around in my head. I had heard talks of this a long time ago, but Father Power had assured me it was nothing to worry about it. I called him and asked if he knew. He didn't. He said he'd see what he could do. The next day, he called and told me that there was nothing he could do. I'd have to go.

"I'm not going. I'm not dragging all this up again," I said, my voice cracking. I was pacing the floor, tethered by the phone cord.

"Catherine, you have to go."

"I'm not going, that's that."

"Catherine, if you don't go, you'll be put in jail."

I paused in my stomping. "There's nothing you can do?"

"Nothing," he said.

A short time later, Marg walked in. Father Power had called her. She took the papers from me and looked them over.

"I'm not going," I said flatly.

"Catherine, you got through worse than this," Marg said simply. "You're going."

Every day, my trepidation and fear rose until the morning of June 24. I didn't know how I was going to make it to the end of the day. I had no idea what an enquiry was, but the thoughts of police and going to court were scary enough. I didn't know how I could handle listening to them talk about the fire. What would I say? What would I see? How would the children handle it? What would I do if they couldn't handle it? What would

I do if I couldn't handle it? Questions coursed through my veins, pulsating me to the point of near-insanity. Sometimes I wondered if insanity was a better option.

If anyone was looking for a way to scourge me beyond the torture I had already been through, and in many regards was still going through, this was it.

I don't remember walking into the building that morning. I was sitting on a long, cold bench with Ida on one side of me and Eddy on the other. Larry, Neil, and young Eddy, as we now called him after stretching five or six inches past his father, were sitting between Ida and the end of the bench.

The room oozed immensity, coldness, and danger. A gavel banged, startling me to action. Before anything started, I spoke out, "Why are you doing this to us? Can't you leave this alone?"

The judge, who had stopped halfway to his seat with my outburst, completed the motion. He looked at a paper on his desk and then back to me. "Mrs. Linehan, I'm sorry, but there were some questions about the fire that destroyed your home, and this enquiry was called to answer them."

"What kind of questions?"

"Mrs. Linehan, there were lives lost," he started.

"I know that all too well," I said. "They were my children."

"Mrs. Linehan, I'm very sorry for your loss. However, I must ask that you let the proceedings begin."

"Father Power told us we wouldn't have to do this," I said, my voice pleading with him to understand.

"Mrs. Linehan, with all due respect, the Church does not rule the court."

Eddy pulled on my arm, and I laid my face in my palms.

A trapped wild animal wouldn't be as confined as I felt in that moment. I wanted to run. I wanted to go back. I wanted none of this.

People I couldn't remember having seen before were called to the stand. My insides twisted into a knot tighter than I ever thought possible. Every bit of me was seized in tension, coiled beyond the breaking point. I only held as long as the skin didn't explode and leave me in bits that would never be pieced back together.

A fire investigator, the police, and a fireman testified. Then Eddy's name was called. I felt Eddy move beside me, he let go of my arm, and the cool air filled where he'd left. A shiver ran through me.

The judge asked him questions. He told what he'd done, why he'd gone for Jer. "I thought we had lots of time," he said simply and, I noted, defensively. I listened without hearing; the words became disjointed like pieces of a puzzle with handfuls strewn across the table. The words were all there in my head but disconnected, bunched, and scrambled. Time slowed to a crawl, and then he returned to sit beside me.

"Catherine Linehan, please take the stand."

I believe my heart stopped. I couldn't breathe and wanted to throw up at the same time. Eddy patted my arm. I took a deep breath and stood. I faltered on the third step forward on the mile-long walk from the bench to the raised wooden cubicle. But I kept going until I was seated next to the judge.

I didn't want to relive those awful moments out loud, but I had to. It was the law. I told him what I had done, about the door closing. I cried out their names.

"Poor Francis."

"Poor Richard."

"Poor Sharon."

"Poor Harold."

"Poor Barry."

I couldn't go on. I feared the enquiry had broken me. I sobbed and grabbed the sides of my face with my hands. I squeezed until it hurt so much I could focus on that physical pain to bring me back. I breathed deeply and concentrated on only that single act.

Tick.

"Mrs. Linehan, that's enough. You can step down."

I couldn't help but think that "enough" was long ago and he had no idea what the word even meant.

I paused to take a few more deep breaths and brushed the traitorous tears with tissues from the box that the judge offered. I walked as straight-backed as I could manage before collapsing on the seat between Eddy and Ida. The two of them reached for me in unison and linked into my arms. We all stiffened. A sense of betrayal filled me as I knew the others would have been affected by what just happened. I wanted to be stronger for them.

Young Eddy was called up next. The judge asked him if he'd been cooking anything that night. Young Eddy shook his head, then answered no. The judge asked him if he was sure, and Eddy said yes, he was sure.

Eddy talked about getting outside through the door in the porch before realizing what was happening. Then he was unable to get back in. In order to alert those sleeping upstairs, he threw junks of wood that his father had split the day before at the window in the girls' room over the porch. He was unaware of what was transpiring inside the inferno. In desperation, throwing the wood was all he could think to do.

Neil was next. He spoke of Richard being so calm and putting on his pants and sneakers and leaving the room, how he tried to follow right behind him but was driven back and knocked down by flames. He beat the window out, and Larry shattered the glass in the top sash above him. The two had scrabbled down the twelve-foot drop on the side of the house. He'd helped his father take Jer out while sparks rained down on him.

Then it was Larry's turn. I was full sure that this enquiry would bring on a seizure in Larry. I got ready to bolt to the stand no matter the propriety of it. I wanted to protect him from this, though I didn't know how. He, too, asked why they had to be there, but then continued to talk about his escape.

The room was charged with emotion and defensiveness when Ida got up. She'd been through so much, and I wanted to grab her and run. There was no need of this. I rocked back and forth on the hard bench with my hands pinned beneath my thighs and willing this to be over.

But Ida told everything she remembered from the time I shouted out until she got to the hospital. The judge remarked on her clarity, seeming not to believe her. That made me mad. The tension that had eased a notch when I left the stand built again. Three times he asked her about turning on the light. Each time, she told him that she did and that it came on. He asked her about the grounding rod as if she'd know what it was. But she did and told him exactly where it was hooked up. She was so matter-of-fact that the judge commented on her testimony before she returned to her seat.

After Ida finished, the coroner got up. I wanted to cover my ears but knew I needed to be brave enough to listen. The coil tightened another couple of notches inside the torture chamber of me. There were things I didn't want to hear about how my children had died. However, I got a glimpse of solace from his testimony that they had all perished from smoke inhalation. Somehow, it seemed more peaceful.

We were all dismissed a short time later. It was over. At least, it was over for those who didn't live it.

Several weeks passed before we got a written summation of the enquiry. No foul play was suspected. The stove had not been on. There was no cause determined. That was the bitterest pill of all. That did not bring the youngsters back or make things better and, I was sure, had already been determined before we went to court.

What we went through in the courthouse was unnecessary. June 24, 1983, could just as well have been June 24, 1980. The hurt was as unbearable then as it had been three years before.

A few years later, we learned that a brand of dryer like we had was being recalled because of reports of electrical shorts that had led to house fires and deaths. Though we would never know the truth of it in relation to our fire, it answered some questions as to the likely cause.

There was no consolation in knowing.

19

Deep Ruts in Old Paths

Neil had married Trudy Mercer from Whitbourne, and in May 1984 a little piece of my heart regenerated when they welcomed our first grandchild, Shayne. I was tormented at first that he'd end up with feet like Francis or Richard or Barry. Neither me or Eddy could recall any of our families ever having such a condition as club feet, but it had to start somewhere. We believed it started with us. Despite my fears, he was healthy.

The dreariness of life began to shift as he grew up in a house in the same meadow as ours. Love was a mender, a time sorter-outer of sorts. Like a baffed-out quilt is renewed by the bright and colourful fabric laid over its top to make it almost good as new again, Shayne's birth covered our worn-out spirits. The underneath was the same battered and ravelledness of wear and tear, but the outside took on a newness of love and freshness of purpose.

That's not to say that Francis, Richard, Sharon, Harold, or Barry were forgotten, because that was impossible. Their absence was eternally with me; it just wasn't as unbearable, that was all.

Within a few years, Kirsten was born. Then Mary had Scott, and Ida had three girls, Sharon, Stacey, and Shawna. Thankfully, none of them were afflicted with club feet, though I was expecting it to reappear at any time. Me and Eddy looked forward to the days when they'd all gather at the house. The sounds of children's laughter rang through the smothering walls and added a joy that I sometimes felt guilty for. But I found a smidgen of peace in the chaos as the memories of my own children growing up were closer than they had been for quite a while. Though I dreamt of them often, it was mostly of that final night, the fire, and what I could have done differently.

Time also becomes a robber of sorts. Maybe it is how it's meant to be. As hard as I tried to keep memories siloed, filed, and separated, they began to rub and mix and combine as the years went by while pages were written in new stories of children connected to me. And connected to them. The whiff of grief rarely shadowed me outside the bounds of the harbour. Though it was rooted deeply inside me, the outside world knew little of this. My plodding on with life kept the darkest torments hidden, disguised from unknowing eyes.

The grandchildren being around was a blessing as well as a distraction from Eddy's bad news. In 1989, he was diagnosed with late-stage prostate cancer. Eddy wasn't eligible for surgery and would be re-evaluated once he went through radiation treatment and chemotherapy.

That diagnosis took the legs out from under me once again. The word "cancer" is a toxin, a noxious gas that clings to everything it touches, painting wide swaths and uncaring of the burdens anyone already carries. I felt it pile into places within me, expanding and choking memories and warm moments with its nasty, clawing grip.

A sense of impending loss clutched me and added to the one for which there had been no forewarning. One breath at a time was the way through as it had been before.

Eddy's treatments started within days. Radiation was the worst of it. He'd be burnt and raw for weeks with little time for recovery in between. He suffered but didn't complain. I tended on him in any way I could. For the next few years, it was a steady gait of going to appointments, tests, treatments, and follow-ups.

Once he was well enough to have surgery, he decided he wasn't having it, despite the doctors' recommendations.

During this time, young Eddy came home and got married to a Polish girl named Irena Ostafin. Irena's mother died in the months leading up to the event, but they chose to go ahead despite her loss because the plans had already been laid.

They had an old-fashioned wedding in the house. The community got together and made cold plates. Meals were served in the living room and dining room on rows of tables from the community hall. There was a dance in the basement. Mostly everyone from the harbour came.

Anna and Patrick, the last of our grandchildren, would be born in Ontario in the coming years.

Neil and Trudy moved away to Ontario, living close to Eddy and Irena, in 1997. I was gutted once again. Shayne and Kirsten were a fixture at the house, and Shayne spent a lot of time with his grandfather, keeping him company. With them gone, the silence became unbearable, and the tick of the clock could be heard once more. Ida was in college in St. John's, and she usually brought her girls in from St. Bride's to see us each Saturday. Mary was working, and she came home with Scott when she could. But the weekdays were simply lonely.

Eddy's health deteriorated slowly at first. It crept up on him and on us. From time to time I had to bring in wood or light the fire or other small things he had spent his lifetime doing. That didn't trouble me, though. He had a catheter put in 1998 to ease his condition, and antibiotics became part of his daily regimen. He improved and, on good days, returned to going in the woods. He'd tie the urine bag to his leg and go off on the bike to cut a load of wood. He kept himself as busy as he was able with that. The outdoors had mostly been his salve.

He'd had a horse for the woods even before we moved to John's Pond. This meant we'd had a horse for all the years we'd been together. But the last horse, Brenda, had been killed on the road, and Eddy was physically no longer able to provide for another. I'd made, spread, carried, and stowed enough hay to last me a lifetime and wasn't interested in being the primary provider for another horse. Eddy had already given up the sheep. That was a tipping point for him knowing that he couldn't do the things he used to any longer.

But Eddy *had* to get in the woods. So, in the early '90s, the fall after Brenda perished, he bought a used Big Red three-wheeler to replace the horse. Being familiar with bikes from his years as a river warden, this was an easy transition for him.

I'd listen to the bike going and coming. I'd recognize the sound of the motor gearing down on the ridge as he came through the back gap. That was my signal to go out and help Eddy unload the wood from the trailer he towed.

There was usually forty-five minutes between each trip. One day he was gone quite a long time, and I was expecting him to be out much sooner. I got worried and was getting ready to go in along the ridge to find him when I saw him limping out the trail.

His bike had rolled on him when he was heading home with the load of wood. He'd been pinned under it and worked his way out from beneath the bike by digging away snow. Luckily, he drove slow and wore his helmet. That had saved him. The next day, he was covered in the reddest bruising from his toes to his shoulder. It was a wonder he hadn't broken any bones.

He didn't trust the bike much after that, nor did I trust him on the bike then, either. I spent hours in the window watching for him every time he went back in the woods. It was like watching could keep something bad from happening. Though I knew it was useless worry, I couldn't stop myself from the torment.

Neil and Trudy moved back in April of 1999, and the noises of children resounded once more. Neil and Shayne helped Eddy with the wood, and he gave up on the bike. I was grateful for the little peace of mind.

In 1999, Larry married in Ontario, and I saved up a bit of money to go. Ida was working in St. John's and planned on taking the girls along with her. Jos said she was going. It was her sister, Marie, who introduced Larry to Caroline. But despite my best efforts to persuade him, Eddy wouldn't hear tell of going. He said he wasn't feeling well enough. He didn't want me to go, either. He had grown accustomed to the ruttedness of daily life now that woods were no longer doable: sleep, eat, cards, and my caring for him were the new practice.

Marg came every day. Her being there gave me a break. It could be the worst weather that you wouldn't put a dog out in, and Marg would walk up the road and play Queens for hours with Eddy. She was my saving grace. Although I liked to play cards, the "have" of it took its toll. Marg, in a way, kept me sane. Her banter back and forth with Eddy, and her laughter, were a welcomed distraction and noise within the walls.

There was a card game every week at the community hall, and Tom Dalton came over those nights, staying with Eddy to let me go. I worried about leaving him alone and in case something happened to him that could be prevented if I was there. While I'd be gone to Toronto, Trudy and Neil would look after Eddy's meals, and Marg would keep him company for a while during the day.

I had to take a break from the taxing comfort of the rut, rejuvenate if only for a week, and face it again upon my return.

20

Breaks and No Breaks

Sometimes, things are simply hard. Not just a one-time-thing hard that you deal with and move on but a constant barrage of hardness that is akin to being run over by an avalanche. Then, after digging and digging and seeing a distant light of day, the next wave of crushing snow comes and you're digging again, after never having surfaced into the warmth of a day for even a breath.

By focusing on the trials and hardships, it isn't easy to see something else. Though it was difficult, I tried desperately to see the light of something else, no matter how tiny it might be. But it was tough to keep picking myself up only to be knocked down repeatedly. Sometimes the knocks were little and rampant, and sometimes they, as I knew all too well, were catastrophic. However, remembering there is light can make all the difference.

I was going to the church one day to make my way around the Stations of the Cross. This was something we did as a family during the season of Lent. Ida was home and said she'd go with me, so we climbed over the fence, crossed through the well-beaten path in the rushes, and then stopped by the graves before making our way up the lane to the church.

It was a beautiful spring day. The ground was thawing but had the underlying hardness of winter frosts lingering and waiting for the sun to do its work.

The church was cold but not raw, and we went around the Stations in the whispered silence of prayer like any other day in Lent. Once outside, the broody sky was gearing up for what promised to be a mix between freezing rain and snow.

"Do you want to go for a walk in on the ridge to see where Dad has the wood cut?" Ida asked. "There's not supposed to be weather until later."

"Let's go," I said as the two of us left the step and headed to the path behind the church. We hopped a small gully that trickled down the hill, not yet free of the ice clinging to the edges. We climbed the steep hill and stopped at the top to catch our breath while looking out over the harbour. We kept on going until we found where Eddy had piled his wood a few months before.

"We can tell Dad we were in here," Ida said. "Only for it's too much work, we could hide some of it."

I laughed. "Not going at that," I said and shook my head at her.

Ida had a habit of playing tricks on the both of us. We didn't mind, though sometimes I'd be going to kill her for it. She'd called me the April Fool's Day before last and had me hunting the house for a book that wasn't there while she was on a collect call with me from St. John's. Last year, she'd thrown boots over the stairs and shouted April Fool's when I came running. But I couldn't be mad, not with Ida.

We headed toward home in silence enjoying the morning. Eddy would be happy that we'd gone to his cut-out. He'd been feeling poorly after coming down with a cold or a flu. He wasn't as keen to go in the woods as he normally did.

At the bottom of Soaker's Path, before entering the gap in the back meadow, Ida stopped. "Want to go over behind Kenneth's for a walk?" Kenneth was a cousin who lived in the neighbouring house with his wife, Sadie. I nodded, veered, and went ahead of her along the fence and up the hill on the other side of the path. I'd just crested the hill when my foot slipped, and down I went.

Ida was behind me and started to laugh. I got a fright but thought I was all right as Ida ran to me to help me up. When I turned over to put my feet under me and get up, I noticed the bottom of my leg was in an odd position.

"I think I broke my ankle," I said as I sized up my foot.

"Cripers, Mom, I think you did." Ida was still laughing as she tried to pull me up.

We struggled together to get a position that I could use one leg to leverage myself up. Finally, I stood, and Ida squeezed in under my arm to help me.

"I can't move," I said. "There's no way you're going to get me out of here by yourself."

Ida looked for a stick to keep me up, but there was nothing close. I grabbed the top of a small tree by the side of the path. That kept me balanced on one foot while I held the other up off the ground.

"You have to go get your father," I said. "See if one of the Trembletts are home to help him, and knock off laughing." The Trembletts lived on the other side of Kenneth and Sadie.

"I can't help it," Ida managed to say. She was laughing hysterically now. "I'll get help." She turned and bolted down the hill and out of sight.

"Don't fall," I shouted after her.

"I won't," came the laughing reply.

I stood holding the tree and watched the path. How was I going to get out? Eddy wouldn't be able to carry me. I hoped Ida would find somebody to help her father, as she wouldn't be able to do it after only recently having surgery on her arms.

There was still no sign of Eddy, and Ida had been gone long enough to be home. I started imagining things like she'd fallen and was knocked out somewhere between me and the house. I had all kinds of thoughts racing through my head as I frantically searched for something that might help propel me down the hill. I was about to sit down and pull myself along the ground with my hands and good leg when Eddy finally appeared on the path.

He was beat out by the time he got to me. "Where's Ida gone?" I asked.

"She went to Tremblett's. She was laughing, and I wouldn't believe her. I wasn't going to come in."

Within moments, Adrian burst through the trees looking for me. I was so thankful he came, because Eddy wouldn't have been able to get me out. They stood on either side of me, and I hopped along on one foot, that one rarely touching the ground as Adrian bore my weight. We got to the top of the meadow and out of the woods when my nephew Johnny saw us. He was on his way to the mail.

Adrian called to him for help, and in no time, they'd made a chair for me by linking arms and were carrying me into the house. Once they got me on the daybed, Adrian, who'd been babysitting, went home to let Ida come back.

Johnny rolled towels and fitted them around my leg. He wouldn't let Eddy take off my boot. Ida called around and got somebody to take me to Placentia to the cottage hospital. Ida went with me, and she was still laughing.

Just as we were about to get aboard the car to go, down came the freezing rain. It encased everything. The road became treacherous in a matter of minutes. The ride to the hospital was slow and dangerous as the car slid from one side to the other and struggled up hills on the way. But we made it without incident.

Although I couldn't understand it, the X-ray showed my ankle had shattered. It had been a simple fall, and I had no pain, but they said they couldn't do anything with it there. Before long, I was in an ambulance with Ida headed for the Health Sciences Centre in St. John's. The roads were now like a skating rink.

At the hospital they cut off my boot and my jeans and fitted my leg in a blow-up cast to wait for the swelling to go down. I was operated on the next evening and had several pins put in and my leg casted in the traditional white plaster. After a few days I got fitted with another cast, and I was allowed to go home to recuperate.

The next six weeks went by slowly. I didn't like to be im-mobile. It was bad on the mind. The nurse came to check on me a few times, Mom and Marg passed the time with me, and Ida took on the household chores.

I was home a week when Eddy wanted bread baked. He was no stranger to making bread. He'd done it himself almost every day when he worked in the logging camps in Badger, but Ida said she wanted to learn.

Under Eddy's guidance, she started. His first instructions were to add lots of water. She did that. By the time Ida was finished, Larry had to go next door for flour, Trudy brought in everything she had, and Larry had to go to the shop for another bag. She baked twenty-six pans of bread that day using both our own and Trudy's oven.

"Go big or go home," was all she said when the last pan was emptied on the table, and she smiled proudly.

"That's what you get for laughing at me."

Ida laughed again. "Probably," she said.

By the time the six weeks were up, I was getting stir-crazy. I wanted to be done with the cast. I'd knit and I'd read and I'd played cards and I wanted to blow the dust from the house off me. Finally, the time came for it to be over. I went to Placentia to have the cast removed.

An X-ray showed the bone had healed and the pins had set. I was taken to the cast room to have the heavy plaster cut off. After two cuts of the saw, I was ready. I knew it would feel a bit awkward at first, but I had my extra sneaker with me and couldn't wait to put my foot to the floor once again.

When the technician grabbed hold of the cast, it wouldn't budge at first. So, he leaned in and gave it a mighty yank. I came off the chair with a scream. Blood and pus and water flicked everywhere, and every bit of my leg below the knee throbbed and stung to form a vicious pain.

The technician ran from the room and returned with a

doctor and nurse moments later. I fell back in the chair and writhed in pain.

The doctor took one look at me. "Cast blisters," he proclaimed. "Oh my, we very rarely see those."

My leg was black and purple. It oozed a grimy liquid, and the pain was immense. Over the next hour, though it felt like days to go through it, my leg was bathed, cleaned, coated in an antibiotic cream, and bandaged. The pain ebbed to bearable, though I refused medication.

"It is similar to a severe burn," the doctor said absently as he taped the last of the bandage. "It is really a rarity." Thoughts of the children flashed through my mind, and I had to brace myself to stop them.

I was sent home with strict orders to keep my leg elevated for at least six weeks, and a nurse would visit daily to monitor my progress. The only thing going through my mind was that Ida had come through her burns without complaint, and I was determined to mirror her attitude.

My leg didn't heal well, and I continued to need medical treatment past the six-week mark. It would be ten weeks before I was finally able to stand on my own two feet and almost four months after the fall on the hill.

My leg was never the same after that. It swelled and pained frequently. But like everything else, it was something I had to live with. No matter the discomfort, it was good to be able to stand and walk again. Though I had had complexities beyond what many others would recover quickly from, and then more complexities on top of that, I didn't let it get me down. There was no sense to that. No matter what, I'd make the best of the worst of it.

21

Mom and Her Old Man

Every night, with very little exception and no matter the weather, I visited Mom and Dad. I'd leave there as they both were going to bed, and I'd usually get home around ten o'clock. Most of the time I'd dodge the mile up the road on pitch-black nights where only one or two street lights actually shone on the road. I didn't mind. I wasn't afraid, though I'd pass Chapel Hill as well as the church and graveyard on the way. It was a ritual for as long as I could remember.

After Francis got his car, he'd often come get me, if he was around. After the fire, I continued the pilgrimage to and from their place. Sometimes young Eddy would come after me, or somebody going up or down the road would stop for me. I liked the walk, and I couldn't get through a night at home without going to see them. No matter where I was, my mother and father were often on my mind.

In the last few years of their lives, their place had changed from the house that Uncle Bill had owned and left to Mom, the place where we grew up, to a small one-bedroom apartment at the back of Dick and Marg's house. It was just up the road and only a few feet from the house where Mom was born and grew up. My mother didn't go very far, and yet she went as far as she wanted to go.

The original house was old and needed lots of repairs. It hadn't been well-built in the way of a stately home but more slapped together out of necessity sixty or seventy years before. The two stayed as long as they could but made no fuss about the move, simply because they were together.

Mom was quiet and kind, caring nothing for herself but for others. They had a simple life. They'd get their pensions at the end of the month and walk to the shop, arm in arm, to get their groceries. Once she was no longer able to do that, my father stopped going as well. They'd ask one of the grandchildren to do their business at the store, and Marg helped pay their bills. They saved money for their burial, and everything else they gave away.

Mom had the heartiest silent laugh that was a trait of the Powers. She and Aunt Annie's crowd especially were alike. They'd shake uncontrollably when they laughed, and not a sound would come out. Most important of all, Mom liked to laugh.

One day in particular, Ida came from St. Bride's in an old car they owned. She took the notion that day that I'd learn to drive. I got in, and we took Mom with us, all three squatted in the front seat, Ida driving and me on the other side, with Mom in the middle.

We went out of the place, toward Branch, where traffic was scarce. Ida pulled the car to a stop, and we traded places. I was going along quite slow, maybe ten or fifteen miles an hour.

Mom and Ida were talking, and I was leaned forward, death grip on the wheel and concentrating on the road. I was fine coming down the hill, but at the bottom, the potholes were deep and stretched from one side of the road to the other. Most people kept out as far as they could to avoid the worst of them. That day they were full of water, and it was hard to judge the depth of any of them.

I kept over as far as I thought I could, and Ida let out a howl for me to stop. She thought we were going to tumble over the bank and onto the bus that was parked in the meadow below. I slammed on the brake and got mad because she gave me a fright. Mom just shook. She shook until we got home. For days after, when I saw Mom, she'd start to shake as soon as our eyes met. I only attempted to drive once more after that and then gave up on it.

In the last ten years or so of her life, Mom became ill. Marg often called me, and I'd go down. We'd get the ambulance to come for her. My father would look at me and say, "Catherine, you'll go with her, won't you?"

I couldn't say no. I'd get aboard the ambulance with her and be gone, sometimes for up to two or three weeks. I'd stay with May or Mary, pick up a few things to wear at Woolco, and make do. There were times we thought she was dying. We'd sit vigil with her, but she'd rally, and we'd get to take her home. She had an enlarged heart, angina, and an aneurysm in her stomach. The doctors said she could go any time. She'd say she couldn't leave her "old man."

On June 11, 1988, capelin boats were fishing out around Colinet Island. My father was out looking at them most of the day either from Dick's front step or from the living room window. That evening there was Mass in the church, and Mom and Dad stayed home as was their usual routine.

I had gone to work by this time, getting a seasonal job at the fish plant in Admiral's Beach working at the capelin landed there from the boats. The hours could be long, and the fish plant was hard work, but I didn't mind. It was nice to have a bit of money to call my own and to get out of the house. I made some wonderful friends there, too.

I was on the line picking capelin—separating the males from the females—when I got a tap on the shoulder and was told to go to the office for a call. Trudy was on the phone.

When Marg and Dick came home from Mass, Mom had been on their doorstep after coming out around the back of the house. She was crying and said there was something wrong with my father. When Marg and Dick rushed in, he was dead.

Mom said he leaned ahead in the reclining chair by the window, lit his pipe, and looked at her saying, "Ida, I think I'm dying." He sat back and was gone.

I'd gotten home from the plant around ten the night before, and it had been too late to go to see them. I had no way to get home from the fish plant, so Neil and Trudy packed up the youngsters and drove from North Harbour to get me. I sat in that tiny windowless office for several hours tormented about Mom. Though I was sad, my father had lived a healthy and long life, but I knew his death would kill my mother.

Marg said the hearse had been in North Harbour on business at the same time and was notified that my father had died. Within the hour, my father had been taken away.

By the time I got home and changed and rushed to see Mom, she was frantic. I got in the bed with her that night, and she cried because he was gone. I stayed with her for the few days until the funeral was over. The next night, Marg called; Mom wouldn't go to bed unless I was there. I spent a few more nights with her but couldn't keep that up, so I brought her home with me. For the better part of the next two years, she pined for her "old man." She couldn't wait to die.

Her health declined rapidly. First, her legs gave out on her. She could hardly walk more than a few steps. I couldn't leave her alone. Ida came one day, and I wanted to go to the shop. I warned Mom not to go getting up because Ida was pregnant and wouldn't be able to help her. Mom promised she'd stay put at the end of the table.

I walked to the shop and was gone about half an hour. When I got back, Ida was on one knee in the middle of the floor with her other one bent and holding up Mom, who was shaking with laughter. I rushed in and got Mom up and back to the table.

She told me she wanted to dabble in the sink and do a few dishes or something so she'd feel useful. I was furious with the two of them, Ida for letting her get up, and Mom for getting up. When I got over the fright, we all laughed about it.

It wasn't long after that that her legs went altogether. She was confined to a bed in Ida's old room. Trudy helped me manage Mom's care. I got a wheelchair and a commode for her.

Thomas Dalton often brought a salt herring for her when she was feeling particularly miserable. I'd boil it, and she'd eat every morsel before claiming she was "revived."

Mom had pains in her chest one day, and I brought her to the hospital. This time, she had a gallbladder attack and needed surgery. She was only there a week that time, and I was able to bring her home again. After the anaesthetic, her mind wandered in and out. She'd cry for my father and prayed to die almost every time she was lucid. She wanted somebody in the room with her for company or just to ground her to something.

Me and Trudy wheeled her down the road one day so she could see the meadow where her house had been. It was torn down by then, but she wanted to see it, anyway. I believe she thought she was closer to my father there.

Sometimes we'd get her out on the step on a fine day so she could sit in the sun. She'd been a smoker and on a few occasions asked for a cigarette. She'd take a puff and then push it away.

When it all came down to it, she wanted to die, and she couldn't die when she wanted.

In February 1991, she'd get her wish. We'd made a dozen trips back and forth to the hospital with her that winter for one thing or another. The last one, she was kept in at St. Clare's Mercy Hospital. We'd left in a hurry, and on the third day, I needed a few staples to keep me going. I'd been there around the clock since she came in. May had stayed with me one night, and Marg the next, so when May came back, I said I'd run to the mall to get the few things I needed.

I was gone less than thirty minutes, and I got an uneasy feeling. Something was telling me I needed to be at the hospital. I put the things I'd picked up on the nearest shelf and left the store. I got a taxi and raced back. When I was walking along the corridor to her room, Marg came out and motioned for me to hurry. The doctor was with her and pronounced her dead when I walked in the room.

I put my lips to her ear and told her I loved her, and then she was gone. I was relieved for her more than I was sad, as odd as that may sound.

She was where she wanted to be, with "her old man."

22

Hopes for a Better Tomorrow

January 1994 didn't start like a normal year, although maybe it's what my normal had become. What was full of promise and hope for most was filled with dread and worry for me. Though in some ways I guess there was hope, the climb to find it was going to be rocky, and in the end, I was praying that Larry would be cured.

On January 2, Larry was admitted to the Health Sciences Centre in St. John's. It was a place that had become all too familiar to me, like the Janeway had been in the early years. Larry was scheduled for brain surgery in an attempt to, at the best, cure his epilepsy, and at the least, reduce his seizures.

At only thirty-one years old, he had made more trips to the hospital than anyone in the family. That was a mouthful with our track record. He had fallen so often, I didn't know how he hadn't suffered more serious injuries than the scattered broken bones, blackened eyes, or skinned-out knees, elbows, or face (sometimes all of that and more) that he had had.

I was so fearful of Larry hurting himself, and once he started carpentry, falling on a saw, or off of a roof, was foremost in my torment. I was afraid for his life. Always afraid. I could never recall a day without one of those fears or another for Larry. But brain surgery, that eclipsed the worst of them.

After months of going back and forth to surgeons and for tests, bloodwork, pill changes, and more medical procedures, Larry's epilepsy was determined to be caused by scarring on the brain. Larry was to be taken away in the morning, put to sleep, have the cap of his head removed, woken up, and scar tissue removed while the doctors tried to stimulate seizures.

Neil, Mary, and Ida gathered with me at the Health Sciences Centre in a tiny waiting area to see Larry be wheeled off to what I couldn't help but think was his demise. I had my prayer beads circling my fingers as I said rosary after rosary for him. I stayed there quietly praying for hours until a doctor came out and said that they had succeeded with removing the scarring and that time would tell if it was successful.

An orderly came and told us when Larry would be brought up on the floor to a special care unit equipped to closely monitor him post-surgery. He'd be out in the general ward in the coming days depending on how he was progressing.

Every time the elevator dinged, my eyes fixed on the doors and my heart raced. It must have been another hour before the ding yielded Larry. The stretcher rolled out from the silver cavity and into the light of the corridor. Monitors beeped, blood and intravenous ran, bags were strung off the side. It was Larry.

Neil shouted out Larry's name from the chairs by the window, where he sat next to me. Larry pushed his arm in the air and made an answering groaning cheer that told us he was awake. Hope spawned in me, and the tension released enough to let my breathing calm once again.

It would be the next day before I could see him. I telephoned Eddy and told him that Larry had pulled through. He said he wasn't worried, that he was sure Larry would be all right. I could hear relief in his voice despite his words.

We all left the hospital drained from the wait. I went to stay with my sister, May.

I had a restless night expecting the phone to ring at any time with news that Larry was gone. Fortunately, there was no such call. May wanted me to have breakfast before I left, but I couldn't eat. She dropped me off at the hospital, and I anxiously made my way up to the special care unit.

There were strict visiting hours that I hadn't been aware of. I was a few hours too early. One of the nurses took pity on me and let me in for a glimpse. Larry had a turban of bandages encasing his head with tubes running from underneath along his face and drained into a bag somewhere out of sight.

I wanted to cry because he looked so helpless, but I also wanted to rejoice because he'd come out of it, and as the doctor said, time would tell. He was alive. I was grateful. I was guided out of the room moments later. After finding the waiting area just down the hall, I sat by a window and took out my prayer beads.

When the hand hit eleven on the clock in the distance, I jumped up and went to his room. A nurse told me not to worry before I went in. She said they'd changed his bandage and things looked good.

Larry was awake, and again I felt a wave of sadness and relief wash over me. I had to be strong for Larry's sake, so I blinked back the tears as we locked eyes.

"How are you, Mom?" he asked with a hint of grogginess in his voice.

"Never mind me. Are you okay? Are you in pain?" I touched his arm.

He slowly shook his head from one side to the other. "I'm all right, I suppose," he said and attempted to laugh.

I held up my hands for him to stop as fear overtook everything else I was feeling. "Don't move your head. You'll hurt yourself."

He stared up at me and smiled. "I'm all right," he said again.

He told me about his surgery and about being woken up in the middle. "I don't think they could find a brain," he said and tittered. "Maybe that's what's wrong with me."

"Was the doctor in?"

"Not yet. He's supposed to be up soon."

I stared at him then, took in his smile, and thought about all he'd been through.

"I'm all right," he said again. "I'm all right."

The doctor spoke behind me.

"You did just fine," he said. He looked to me, then. "He did well, Mom. All we can do is wait now." He patted my shoulder.

He talked about the surgery. They had removed the scar tissue but didn't know if that was truly the root cause of the seizures.

"It will take time," he said as he left the room.

I had to leave, then, because my hour was up. "I'll be back from two to three o'clock," I said. I left and went back to the seat by the window and prayed some more.

The second hour, Larry mostly slept. I stayed on a chair by the bed until visiting was over. I told him I'd be back in the morning.

After another sleepless night, the next morning, I was there at eleven. The nurses and doctor were with him, and I couldn't go in.

"What's happening?" I asked at the desk.

"The doctor will be out momentarily," she said as she smiled.

The first thought that raced through my head was that he was dying. I couldn't help but think the worst. I stayed by the door. I believed I heard Larry's muffled voice, and that relieved a tiny notch of tension. There were more voices, and one of the nurses came out. The doctor caught sight of me and motioned for me to go in.

With tentative steps, I passed the washroom and pushed back the edge of the curtain. Larry was in a sitting position in the bed.

"Your son had a seizure, Mrs. Linehan. But I want you to know that that is to be expected." He looked at me reassuringly and then at Larry.

"You've just had surgery. Your body sees that as a serious trauma. We can't tell if this seizure is merely a symptom."

"How long before we know?" I asked. My heart, which had been pounding in my chest, began to slow.

"I can't tell you that, Mrs. Linehan. Time needs time. That's all I can say for sure."

The next day when I got to Larry's room, the nurse told me he was on the ward now. I took that to be a good sign. Over the next days, he was released, and he came home to recuperate.

He had an odd seizure here and there, but nothing like the almost daily ones he had had in the past. Over time, and with changes to medication, Larry wasn't cured, but he was considerably better.

That was the best we were going to get after time had its time.

23

My Life's Partner

In September 1998, I traded in the rubber boots of the summer in the fish plant for my old-age pension. I was able to stay home with Eddy, who by this time was in a steady state of decline. Though he wasn't able to go in the woods like he used to, he managed to go out around the door and pick at one thing or another on his good days. The trouble was his good days were getting fewer and fewer.

With the catheter, he'd have infection after infection, or worse, blockages. We made multiple trips to Placentia or in the ambulance to St. John's for double doses of antibiotics when the daily one would not knock down the bacteria. His cancer had spread, and he was miserable most of the time, though he said nothing.

He still loved playing cards. Marg was a constant at the house. Neil and Trudy and the kids had returned, so between us all, we kept him occupied. Thomas Dalton visited just about every night to keep him company. They'd yarn and reminisce of days gone by and those who'd gone before them.

When we were alone, Eddy often lay on the daybed and snoozed or sang off-key songs from his time in the lumber woods in Badger. When he stayed in bed late and sometimes didn't get up at all, I did what I could for him to make him comfortable until he'd give in to my urgings and go to the hospital.

One day, he was raving so bad I thought I would lose him. The community care nurse came, assessed him, and called the ambulance. He said the only thing that saved him during that time was taking sight of the corner of the dresser with the wallpaper border like he would if he was hunting. That kept the room from spinning and let him know he was alive.

His appointments became more frequent with the cancer doctors. Every few weeks, we had to go to St. John's. Sometimes he'd have procedures or tests, and then we'd go home.

One day, Ida brought us out for an appointment. When it was over, he said he was hungry and wanted a slice of toast and a cup of tea. We'd been on the go early, so we went to the Avalon Mall to eat. He was doubtful there'd be tea and toast there, but Ida told him not to worry.

We walked through the lower part of the mall to catch the escalator to the food court. Eddy went first, and Ida was behind him. Before I stepped on the moving stairs, I realized something had gone terribly wrong. Eddy had grabbed the non-moving part of the escalator, and while his feet and legs went up, the rest of him stayed still.

Ida, who'd been standing beside him, quickly moved and stepped on the tread beneath his back. She pried his hand from the metal and placed it on the moving rail, she too now tipping back. As he was going up the escalator, almost lying flat, she walked one step at a time behind him, pushing him up until he was standing, just in time to get off. I was still at the bottom, mouth open.

I met them at the top, red as a beet, imagining all the things that could have gone wrong. I got Eddy a spot to sit, and I collapsed beside him, the fright slowly wearing off. Within five minutes, Ida came back with tea and toast from one of the restaurants. Eddy smiled, never acknowledged what had happened, and ate. Ida and I took turns staying at the table with him while the other went off to get food and return.

At another appointment a few weeks later, we were invited to my sister, May's, for lunch. He wanted tea and toast again. I linked arms with him now wherever we went, because he had become unsteady on his feet and was stumbling and fumbling around. Eddy went in ahead of me through the hall, and when he got in the open space going toward the table, he didn't realize nor see that there was a step in front of him. He tripped and went headfirst under the table. Luckily, he didn't break any bones on the hardwood floor.

Between the cancer, infections, and fumbling, he needed constant monitoring at this point. I made sure either I was with him all the time or somebody else was there.

Just before his eighty-fourth birthday the following year, he had to be hospitalized again. This time, we were given the horrible news that his kidneys were failing and that the cancer had metastasized from his prostate to his liver and into his bones. He was given six months to live at the most.

This was a shock. Though I knew it was coming, for the doctors to say it was another thing. The doctor took me aside and told me that Eddy would be in a lot of pain in the coming months. There was a procedure they could do to relieve strain on the kidneys if we were adamant and insistent. But to do it was not recommended because of his age and given his health. The doctor said that for his kidneys to shut down, it would be a more peaceful end for him.

Up to that point, he had no extra discomfort that he made me aware of, nothing to suggest this news. According to the doctor, the decision would have to be made in the coming week.

I told him that I'd talk to Eddy about it and let him decide. We went home for a few days, and the decision was taken away from us. Eddy stumbled out of the room, sat on the arm of the couch, and asked me to call the ambulance.

This was the first time he'd ever done that. It had usually been a plea from me for him to go. Eddy said something was different and he had new pain. On top of that, before the ambulance arrived, his catheter stopped working and he was having a hard time of it.

At the Health Sciences Centre, he was quickly assessed and was admitted. However, there were no beds available. He was to be kept in emergency all night.

Since I wasn't allowed to stay there, I went to Mary's for the night, and Ida said she'd go see him in the morning on her way to work.

When the phone rang the next morning, I expected Ida to say that he was okay and had gotten a room. Instead, she told me he'd had a procedure done overnight. I got ready, and Mary drove me in to the hospital.

Eddy was still on a stretcher in a room at emergency. He was asleep, on his side, when I got there. There was a tiny tube sticking out of each side of his back. I assumed, and a nurse confirmed, that they were coming from his kidneys.

Eddy's cancer doctor held clinics in the same hospital, so I went there and asked the secretary if the doctor could come by to see Eddy. I told her that I had questions about his surgery. I left to return to Eddy, expecting the doctor would be over by the end of the day, but within minutes he walked in behind me.

"Mrs. Linehan," he said, accompanied by a quick nodded acknowledgement as he grabbed the chart from the slot at the foot of the bed.

I stared wide-eyed at him, partly with surprise, and partly waiting for him to finish reading.

"I thought we discussed your husband's outcome from this procedure," he said, his tone holding a hint of defensiveness as he glanced up at me and then back at the paper.

I didn't speak, because I didn't connect what we had talked about a few days before with whatever had happened to Eddy overnight. He must have seen my confusion, because he went around me and examined Eddy's back. Since Eddy was still asleep, the doctor shook him awake and asked how he was doing.

Eddy's raspy voice and grogginess drew me around in front of him. I gave him a sip of water when the doctor nodded assent.

"Mr. Linehan, you had surgery. How are you doing?"

"I think I'm all right," Eddy said as he tried to focus on me and then the doctor. The doctor gave him a cursory examination and then gestured with his brows for me to go outside. I tucked the sheets around Eddy and followed him through the door.

"Mrs. Linehan, you realize what this means?"

"I realize nothing," I said. "I don't know what happened." My face was blank of emotion as I stared up at him waiting for him to tell me.

"Mrs. Linehan, your husband will have a few hard and painful months ahead."

"Okay," I said. "Is there anything I can do?"

"You know he had the surgery we talked about, right?"

"What surgery? Eddy came in because his catheter had stopped. He was in pain. I don't know what they did to relieve it."

He looked at me under his eyes. "You didn't ask for this?"

"My daughter called me this morning and told me to come in. She said her father had something done overnight. That's all I know."

He sized me up again, his eyes evaluating my demeanour. "I'll be back shortly," he said as he swivelled and strode down the hall.

A little while later, I heard voices coming into range, and one of them was Eddy's doctor. I sat straighter in the chair. A fellow in a white coat switched on the lights that I'd turned off minutes before.

I listened to the doctor talk and got bits of "they hadn't decided" and "did you ask" and "that's not the best outcome" before all left but for Eddy's doctor, who sat on the edge of a chair and leaned toward me.

"In simple terms, Mrs. Linehan," he said as he held the rail of the bed and stared over it at Eddy, "your husband's prostate is enlarged to the point that it's affecting his urine output, and there is nothing we can do. They performed an emergency procedure last night to relieve the strain on the kidneys. We won't know if it worked for a few days. As soon as there is a bed, he'll be sent upstairs."

I nodded that I understood, and he left. By that evening, Eddy was doing much better. He was admitted and moved to a room on the fifth floor. It was a large and odd-shaped place with six beds, and Eddy was wheeled in the corner with his head near the door. The space was quite crowded but was better than the emergency room. I went to Mary's that evening after getting a lunch of tea and toast for Eddy.

The next day, he was in good spirits.

"How are you feeling, Dad?" Ida asked.

He gave her a brilliant smile and said, "I got a few years left in me yet."

By evening, he was tired early and went to sleep after supper. I waited with Mary for a few hours, then left for the night. When I returned in the morning, the doctors had been in. Eddy's cancer doctor came by around noon. After giving Eddy a quick exam, he asked me to step outside with him.

"Mrs. Linehan, the kidney procedure hasn't worked out for your husband."

I nodded and waited, not knowing what I was expecting

him to say. "Will you take out those tubes? When can he go home?" I asked.

"Your husband is in kidney failure."

I didn't know what that meant. I waited for him to explain the next steps, but he didn't. He sized me up for a few seconds, then said, "At the last appointment, I explained that if he had the procedure he might get five or six months more, but he'd be in terrible pain."

I nodded again.

"That's no longer an option, and his kidneys are shutting down." He paused then, knowing I wasn't fully understanding. "Mrs. Linehan, if anyone is away and wants to see him, they should come sooner rather than later."

"Is he dying?" I asked bluntly as I quieted the unease rising in my stomach.

"We can't say how long, but it's a matter of days and not weeks that we're looking at. If it is any consolation, it will be a peaceful ending."

His pager beeped. He glanced at it and turned to me. "I'll be back again later this afternoon to check on him." He turned and left me there in the hall, stunned by the news. Larry and young Eddy had to be told so they could come home. Mary, Neil, and Ida as well.

Eddy and Larry caught a flight later that morning and were expected in by six. When Ida went to the airport for them, they weren't on the flight. She came back to the hospital, and I thought they'd be behind her.

"They didn't get in," Ida said. "It won't be until tomorrow now."

"I don't believe you," I said as I tried to look around her, expecting the boys. "I know they are there somewhere."

"Honest to God," she said.

"I don't believe you. You're codding me."

"Does this look like a time to be kidding around?" Ida asked. Her serious face told me she wasn't joking.

"Really?"

"Yes, I was out waiting, and they didn't show up. I called, and they're not getting in until tomorrow at the same time."

I looked at Eddy. He'd barely woken throughout the day. He wasn't eating or drinking. I hoped he'd hold on until the boys got home.

Thomas Dalton came to see him later that evening. Ida kept after her father until he acknowledged his dearest friend. Thomas was quiet in the chair as he sat with Eddy. I'm sure there were lots of memories flowing through his mind and in the air that he stared at. When he got up to leave, Thomas stood by Eddy and placed his hand on Eddy's shoulder. He gave him a nudge and turned and left with his daughter, who'd come to get him.

Marg, my old faithful friend, had come in earlier that day and stayed there with me during the night. Mary, Neil, and Ida went home to their kids. Eddy woke twice during the night for mere moments, and I gave him a sip of water each time. We took turns swabbing his mouth to make him comfortable. We remained quiet because of the others in the room.

The next day, Eddy hardly woke at all. The doctor said he could hear us, though he couldn't speak. I prayed young Eddy and Larry would make it. My prayers were answered when they walked into the room that evening. Eddy woke for a few minutes and recognized them before drifting off once again.

Young Eddy, Neil, and Trudy stayed with Eddy that night. I went with Mary to lie down and returned in the morning. I don't know how much, if any, sleep I got because I was expecting a call to go to his side. But there had been no change in him. Family gathered again while Neil and Trudy went to Mary's for some rest.

Everyone took turns coming in and going out to the waiting area so as not to overcrowd the room. The other four patients had visitors, too, and with Eddy next to the door, we were often in the way of people entering and exiting.

The doctor checked on us and said they were trying to find a private room, but nothing was available right then. The nurses moved Eddy back and forth from lying on his right side to his left side several times that morning. He hadn't made a sound since we got there.

We took turns swabbing the inside of his mouth and his lips with sponges to make him comfortable. I don't know if it worked, but it made us feel useful to him.

Around noon, I got up and went to the rail of his bed. I leaned in on him for a few minutes, feeling his warmth and listening to him breathe. His breaths were shallow with a long time between each one. I stood by the rail when, all of a sudden, Eddy grabbed my arm and sat up. He stared up at the ceiling.

Ida jumped up and came to the other side of the bed.

"He's dying," I said frantically. "Ida, get someone!"

Ida bolted for the door and shouted for the nurses who were behind a desk across the hall. She came back in and grabbed his other hand. Two nurses rushed in. One went around me to Eddy's side.

"Don't let go of him. It's all right. You're not in my way," the nurse said as she raised the head of the bed to support Eddy's back. The other nurse left and returned with whoever was waiting in the family room.

Eddy clutched me tightly, and I rested my other hand on his forearm as the nurse put her stethoscope to his chest. She leaned in to listen above the commotion in the room. Eddy held on to me and Ida while the others touched his legs and feet. Gradually, his grip loosened, and I knew he was gone before the nurse confirmed it with a gentle nod and a touch on my shoulder. She lowered the head of the bed, and Eddy went with it.

I don't know what I was in that moment. Everyone began crying and hugging one another. Strangers looked on. I laid Eddy's hand on the bedsheet and leaned in over him once more. I touched his face and smoothed his forehead. I straightened the medical gown and pulled the sheet up and tucked it around his arms. This was the final time I'd feel his warmth, and I wanted it to last.

I squeezed his hand one last time and moved out around the bed. All the children embraced me in their turn. I held them tight as they cried. The boys went off somewhere, each one alone, I was sure. Ida's girls hugged my legs, and I patted them on the head.

We all stood there, then. Strangers intruded on our gathering, coming and going through us and behind us. My biggest torment was I didn't know what was next. Did we leave him there? Would somebody tell us to go? I wasn't thinking about my husband having just died but of what was next. I was caught once more in the habits of death.

I went back to Eddy's bedside and laid my hand on his forehead once more. I whispered a prayer. I moved to the foot of the bed and stared at him.

"I don't know what I'm supposed to do now," I said aloud to nobody in particular. I thought a nurse or a doctor would be there to give us direction.

Stacey, Ida's middle girl, grabbed my hand. "Nan, I'll tell you what to do," she said with profound sincerity as her wide brown eyes caught mine. "We'll take Poppy home and bury him behind a tree. Pop would like that."

"Pop would definitely like that," I said as I choked back a sobbing laugh. I smoothed her hair and then kissed the top of her head.

Mary asked the nurse to come back and answer my question.

"You stay here as long as you want," she said. She pulled the curtain around us. "Let the funeral home know, and they'll take care of the rest."

"So, we just walk away?"

"Yes, when you are ready."

"I didn't see Shayne," I said.

"He went down for coffee," young Eddy said.

"He doesn't know!"

"I'll go get him," Ida said and left the room.

Shayne was in tears when he walked in. He went to his

grandfather and hugged him. Everyone started crying again, except for me. As the mother and grandmother, it was up to me to be strong for them all. It was something I'd gotten used to, I guess.

Mary called Neil and Trudy but couldn't reach them at her place. She asked a neighbour to get them up and tell them to come to the hospital.

Once Neil and Trudy came and said their goodbyes, we left shortly after. I looked back at the closed curtain as strangers stared at me from around the room. I called Marg and told her. She said she'd take care of notifying Dunphy's Funeral Home.

The weather had been miserable up to that point with record-breaking snowfalls predicted to be the highest in a hundred years. Every day there'd been snow, which meant it was hard to get around. Young Eddy volunteered to go out to North Harbour and get his father's suit. He'd drop me up to May's and take me to the funeral home once he got back.

After the first business part of dying was done, we went home to North Harbour to wait. With snow everywhere, I didn't know what we were going to do about the church and the grave. It was a useless worry. People showed up. The grave got dug, the driveway was plowed, and the path to the gravesite was cleared.

For the next three days, the sun shone brilliantly, the wind died out, and Eddy rested in the wake room attached to the back of the church. With so many things to attend to, greetings to make, welcoming friends and family, talking to people, and accepting condolences, it didn't sink in that Eddy had died.

During the day, the kids went sliding on the hill just outside the door of the wake room. Their giggling and laughter rang out through the church, and though the staunch believers in propriety didn't approve, I knew that Eddy would. He loved the children.

Several times the kids would burst in through the door full of snow and runny noses. They'd go up to their grandfather and look at him before getting their noses wiped, their clothes fixed up, their boots adjusted, and go back to sliding on the hill. Somebody would go behind them with the mop, and then they'd repeat.

I think the simplicity of it all, and the grandkids around, kept me calm and got me through it. Although I knew it was coming, that Eddy was dying, it was different when it finally happened. He'd suffered so much without complaint, especially over the last couple of years. My sole consolation was that he hadn't suffered in the end.

The church was full the next day at his funeral. The wheels on the bier squeaked as he was brought out. The choir sang. I walked through the path in the snow to the same plot I had walked to over twenty years before.

The shock this time was as different as was the management of it. The man I'd loved and married almost forty-eight years before was laid to rest beside Francis. He'd be the first to see our other five again. I was and continue to be as certain of that as I am of breathing. That was the solace in the sadness of parting.

Once the prayers were over, there was a reception in the nearby hall, as was the new custom in the evolving state of death. The community nobly rallied around us, fed us, cleaned up after us, and went home. I went home, too, a widow at sixty-seven years old.

Bad weather closed in once more. The long and dreary winter unfolded as predicted with its record-breaking snowfall.

24

The Aftermath of Death and Debt

In the days following Eddy's death, I was aware of three things: Eddy was gone, his burial had to be paid for, and I was not staying in that house by myself. The three weren't equally weighted but came with a burden that seemed all too often to hang over me.

I was afraid that if I stayed there alone, without something to keep me busy and my thoughts occupied, I would be driven to insanity within days. I could find something to do in the daytime, but the nights would be hard. The house didn't hold the warmth of precious memories. It held smothering walls, roosting memories of loss, ghosts of those who should still be here, and too much empty space.

Shayne was in high school when his grandfather died. It wasn't even a question or a choice for him; he stayed with me to finish out his school years. But I knew that was a temporary thing with a time limit. Shayne would go to college the next September, and the thoughts of the looming nights, which were stalking and circling me from a distance now, would be upon me. I decided to put it out of my head and deal with things as they unfolded. That's what had gotten me through so far.

In the weeks after his death, there was the matter of Eddy's funeral. That had to be paid for. We had no money; it was not something we'd ever had. I often said if I had $20 to spare, there would be something that came along by the end of the day to take it, and I wasn't wrong. That something came, at least more often than I had the $20.

There was one time for a fleeting moment I'd had money when the children were small. It was at the time that the first family allowance cheques came out in the spring of the year. I remember opening the envelope and gasping at the amount. My name was on it, and the amount was way over $1,000. I allowed I had more money than the Queen of England as I gazed at the numbers on the left of the decimal. I felt like it was true.

That evening after supper, I went to the shop and asked Jos to make up my second bill. That was the one that had the things like kids' school clothes, school supplies, money for fares to medical appointments, and things that weren't part of the monthly grocery bill.

Jos sat by the table and went through the pages of our bill, the things that were on the back of the books, and all the items that accumulated faster than the bit we managed to pay on them every month. When she told me the amount, I looked at the cheque and realized it was one dollar short of the total owed. That dollar was carried over until the family allowance came the next spring. We were fortunate in so many respects to be able to carry things at all.

In the end, the only things I had of any kind of monetary value in the eyes of a financial authority was the old-age pension and the house. I sat down with Marg, and we looked at every possible way to pay Eddy's funeral expenses, and it continuously circled back to the house.

Up to a few years before that, we'd never had a bank account or any dealings with a bank. Our pension cheques were cashed at the store, our groceries were bought there, any other dealings were cash, and if we were short, Jos would see us through to cheque day.

The equity on the house was how it had begun: a credit card to establish credit and a small mortgage to get new windows and siding for the house. The wooden ones were rotting and needed to be changed. Now it was a remortgage to pay off Eddy's funeral expenses and get a headstone with a little left over to get me situated. I'd make payments from my pension, and all would be right with the world, in a perfect world. I was living in something that was far from perfect. Under no circumstances was I worldly in any sense of the word. I had been sixty-five when I went to Larry's wedding in Ontario, an enormous feat in my eyes, as it was something I'd never dreamt possible.

Over the years, I'd been invited to travel with May and her husband, Cecil, or with Marg and Dick, but I had normally had a reason not to go. Either my mother was sick, or Eddy was sick, and accompanying that, the main reason was I had no money.

When the house had burned in 1980, I had hoped Eddy would agree to move to St. John's instead of building back in North Harbour. Although I never really knew if this was something I wanted, and I didn't speak it out loud, I imagined it was and that I had. Maybe it was a wish, or a hope, but to me after Eddy died, it was real.

Though I loved North Harbour and especially liked the people and had wonderful friends there, the cloud of loss clung to me and hovered and battered me like the bands of an everlasting storm with its eye in the graveyard only a few hundred feet from the house. I don't know if I thought I could outrun the veil of tragedy somewhere else, but the belief that I might propelled me to thinking St. John's could do that for me. Though thoughts that the loss would be more present for me in North Harbour than somewhere else was a foolish idea, the fact that I could be anonymous in that loss had an appeal. I could move about without notice. In North Harbour, everyone knew; somewhere else, very few knew. I thought that maybe getting away would make a difference, and for once there was no stake in the ground tethering me there.

I believed I liked the city of St. John's, though it had been fifty years since I lived there, back when I was in my late teens. The city itself had been a centre of activity for us when the children were growing up, at least a medical one, for sure. Then post-fire, with all of Ida's surgeries and Larry's appointments and surgery, and later still when Eddy got the cancer diagnosis and needed treatments, St. John's had figured prominently in our lives. To look back when truth is most often clearer, it made the most sense, as it is with many things in retrospect when you have lived through one choice or another. But a choice was made when rational thoughts hadn't been foremost on anyone's mind, and the foundation for the new house had been laid, sealing the decision.

With Shayne making plans for life beyond North Harbour, I had to do something. His moving to Ontario in 2003 was a catalyst that drove me to act. It was time to seriously consider leaving. Mary was living in St. John's with her son, Scott, and asked me to come stay with her. I thought I could try it at least until things got figured out in my head. I was quick to agree. My sister May lived there, too, herself now a widow, and I could spend time with her.

In St. John's the September I turned seventy years old, in a small way, I saw the world through unrestrained eyes as I tried to make a new life for myself. The things that I both believed and knew had stopped me no longer existed. There was one thing for sure: I couldn't stay in the house all day, because madness would come to me within the confines of four walls, no matter where they were.

Paying a mortgage and trying to live besides on a small pension was a challenge. The most economical way for me to get out and about was to catch a bus. That was the first thing I'd had to tackle. Scott helped me with that, and St. John's opened to me. The second year I was living there, I went to stay with May for the winter. She was alone, and though she could drive and had a car, she generally stayed home until the spring. It didn't matter to me, as I could get the bus from her place as well as from Mary's, and I didn't want her to be alone. May had been good to me over the years, and in a way, my keeping her company was a way to make reparation for kindnesses I'm sure she'd long forgotten.

When spring came, May was going to make her annual trip to Florida for a month or more, and she asked me to go. Her son lived there and had room for me. My first instinct was no, but my second thought, for the first time, was why not? I remortgaged the house, and I went.

Over the next few years, I would repeat this cycle to go one place or another or sometimes just to keep up with house payments. But soon there was no equity, and I was stuck. The house, after nobody lived there for years, devalued and I quickly sank into financial trouble. By this time, I was eighty. I didn't speak about it to anybody, as it was my trouble, and I didn't want any of my crowd to take that on.

My small Visa exploded and doubled, then tripled with interest, though I was paying what I could on it every month, and the house came due, and I couldn't pay. Then, I couldn't pay again and again. Creditors began calling, and I was way over my head before I realized I was drowning. By then I was dealing with medical issues, which took priority over and compounded the financial woes.

In the end, I was going to lose the house. That used to bother me; no matter how bad off we ever were, I paid my bills. Now, it didn't bother me about the house itself. I didn't care about the house; I hadn't been in it in over ten years. Its weight and reason for being had held me hostage since I walked through its doors in October 1980.

What bothered me was losing the land where my children died and the shame that came with being in such a poor financial state. Despite knowing it was my own fault, that didn't make any difference. The property would still be gone.

To leave this out of my story would be an injustice to the truth, so here it is. At eighty-four years old, the bank and lawyers came after me. The house was put up on bids. Thankfully, for small mercies and many rosaries, Shayne was successful in taking it over. The land would remain in the family.

After the sale was concluded, I thought that was it. But the bank wasn't finished with me. I was given a $24,000 bill for their changing the locks and scrubbing the floors. It will be outstanding when I die.

Hindsight is there to torment you and not to guide you. Choices are made that must be lived with, regardless of their outcomes. In the end, it probably would have come to the same conclusion whether I'd remortgaged the last few times or not at all. The albatross would have looked and felt the same either way. I'd been in over my head from the day that Eddy died, splitting our income in half, unprepared for the costs of not just burying him but doing right by him. The doing right part also comes at a cost.

Nevertheless, life still had to be meandered through while I was on top of the soil. After Eddy died, I had to do that on my own.

25

First Things First

In 2008, Neil and Ida got it in their heads that they would have a "Come Home" weekend in John's Pond to pay tribute to the memory of their father.

"Who do you think is coming home?" I asked when she came up with the idea.

"You never know," Ida said.

"It might fill," Neil said.

"John's Pond was never full," I said. "But if we're going at it, I want to boil dinner on the beach."

Over the next month, they printed invitations and put the word out about the "Come Home" weekend on July 26 and 27.

The week leading up to the big celebration, Ida took her father's scythe and Neil the lawn mower and crossed the ridge into John's Pond. Ida cut the hay, and Neil followed behind to mow the grass, making a place to set up tents on our land. They cleared away the area around the foundation of our old house and got things ready as best they could.

Eddy's nephew David set up a tent, as did Neil and Ida. Mary said she'd go there in the day, but she was only going to sleep in a bed. So, we both stayed at the house and travelled back and forth. I brought a boiler on Sunday and cooked up a feast over an open fire on the beach. We set up a table where the old house had been. Everyone sat around and enjoyed the meal. It was the first time I'd sat down to dinner in John's Pond in over forty years.

Besides the family, almost a hundred people showed up that afternoon. Some had roots in John's Pond, and others just came along to enjoy the day. It turned out to be a great time and a lovely day.

Back at the house that evening, Ida spoke up. "You're going to think this is odd, but walking back from John's Pond, I had something come over me."

"What?" Trudy asked as she laughed.

"Honest to God, I was looking down at my feet, and this weird thought popped into my head."

"Okay," I said. "What was it?"

"It came to me to climb Gros Morne. Honest. I've never even seen it, and it was like a vision."

"Well, are you going?" Trudy asked.

"Yes, I'm going to climb it on Friday."

"Well, if you're going, I'm going," Trudy said.

"Well, if you two are going, I'm going," I said. We all laughed as if we'd just decided to go to Florida somewhere.

Thursday morning, we left the house to make the ten-hour trek across the Island. "We must be after getting foolish," I said as we stuffed a tent and sleeping bags in the trunk of the car.

"Sure, what odds," Ida said. "It's better to be foolish than crooked."

This was my first time to go so far afield. Neil and Trudy had taken me and Eddy around communities as far west as Clarenville when Eddy was looking for people he'd known in Badger. But after Clarenville, everything was new to me.

We stopped a few times to break up the drive, but not for long. As Ida kept saying, we were on a mission and had to get to Gros Morne long before dark. By five that evening, we pulled into a park in Norris Point, and between us all, we set up a tent and sleeping bags, then went looking for bears.

It was a very random thing. None of us had seen a bear before, and there were talks that there were bears in the dump near Rocky Harbour. On our way to find a restaurant, we dropped by the dump.

As we pulled up and lowered the car windows to size up the situation, Ida squealed, then we squealed, as this black animal bounded toward us. At first glimpse we all thought it was a black bear. A man was walking in front of the car, and Ida shouted for him to watch out for the bear. The man laughed as his black dog came through the high grass and wagged his tail at us.

"Where you ladies from? Haven't you ever seen a dog before?"

"St. John's," Ida said quickly, and her glance told us not to contradict her. "We thought it was a bear."

The man was local, so Trudy asked about a good place to eat. Once we got directions, we easily found the place. Because it was late, there were few customers. The server laughed when we told her about thinking the dog was a bear.

Back at the tent just after dark, Ida pulled the car close to the tent door. "We'll leave it unlocked in case a bear comes," she said, her fixation on the animal evident in her tone.

We played cards for a little while inside the dome, then decided to get some rest. It had been a long day in the car. I got in the sleeping bag and tried to turn over but couldn't. I unzipped it, fixed it again, and snuggled in. It was my first time to ever sleep in a tent.

I woke to Ida's shout of "bear" and tried to sit up. I was wound like a corkscrew and couldn't move. My heart raced, but in the dim light of the moon through the canvas, Ida and Trudy made soft snoring sounds. I didn't hear any rustling or growling, so I lay back down again. I unwound myself and got comfortable once again. I believe I slept with one eye open.

The next morning, Ida swore she didn't shout "bear." Maybe I dreamt it, or she dreamt it, I don't know, but I thought she'd been fooling with me and actually did shout "bear."

We made tea and toast on the camp stove that Trudy had packed. We stowed our belongings in the tent and by seven were headed to the national park.

The girls wouldn't let me take a knapsack. They packed water and snacks for the three of us in theirs. Following the signs, we set off to climb the mountain. It took over an hour to get to the base, and the terrain was easy.

People passed us going in, and many remarked on my being there, asking how old I was. "She'll be sixty-nine next month," Trudy or Ida would say proudly. I got lots of high-fives and congratulations for attempting the climb.

At the base, Trudy asked if I was sure I wanted to go up. It didn't look too bad and wasn't what I'd expected, but I was happy to go on. We started up the shaley face of Gros Morne. We took lots of breaks, drank water, and moved on. Lots of people passed us, and as the morning dragged into noon, we reached the summit.

I was tired, but overall, I felt good. "It's all downhill from here," I said as we ate a light lunch near the distance marker that proclaimed we were 806 metres above sea level. The trail continued and circled around the mountain to come out at the base where we started the climb.

We took our time. Trudy snapped some photos as we began the descent. An endless set of stairs on the back side of the mountain made us glad we'd gone in the direction we had and were going down them instead of up. The trail became more rugged than on the face, and it was harder to get along. I grew tired, so we stopped more often.

Ida and Trudy helped me across and around giant boulders. One time I thought my leg was going to go backwards, and I nearly twisted it but saved myself at the last second. Ida and Trudy kept urging me to take my time, so I did.

"We have lots of time," Trudy would say. "It won't be dark until nine."

"Well, if I'm in here at nine, a helicopter will have to come for me," I said.

"It's only three o'clock," Ida said. "We have lots of time."

"Wasn't it three o'clock a long time ago?" I asked.

"No, it's three now." That was said several times in the coming hours, and I didn't have my watch.

After ten hours on the trail, we emerged in the parking lot just after 6:00 p.m., tired and accomplished. We went to the same restaurant we'd dined at the evening before. The server recognized me and gave me a big hug when she heard I'd finished the hike.

"You're an inspiration," she kept saying. She gifted me with a pin that said I CLIMBED GROS MORNE. She fastened it onto my T-shirt and told all the other customers that I'd been on the mountain that day. When it came time to leave, she wouldn't let anyone pay for my supper.

"It's on the house, my dear," she said. "You deserve it."

We went back to the tent and changed out of our sweaty clothing. Within minutes we were tucked into our sleeping bags, didn't care about a bear, and knew nothing till morning. We were all exhausted. Bright and early, we packed up our belongings, took down the tent, and booted it for home.

We stopped in Deer Lake for breakfast before crossing the Island. In three days I'd been in the car for twenty hours, climbed a mountain, slept in a tent, and was back in my own bed on the third night.

It was a whirlwind and an unforgettable trip. Trudy submitted the picture of me standing by the summit sign to the local paper. I became front-page news on September 8, 2002, the week before my sixty-ninth birthday.

26

Riverbeds and Roots

Looking back, I've learned that time can be a friend or foe. It all depended on how I spent it and what I did with it. Sometimes it was difficult to take either one of them, each having equal weight, the friend and the foe.

When I moved to St. John's, I didn't really do anything that first month as I became acclimatized to the reality of starting over. I stayed put. But a crushing weight of loneliness and too much time for thinking swirled around me. I realized nothing had changed from before, except for the setting. With Mary working every day and Scott in school, I either had to pass the hours away until they got home, or I had to do something with myself.

Whiling the hours away was not for me, but the strangeness and newness of a city life was, at first, a little daunting. I had to muster the courage to do something. So, on the most miserable weathering days, I'd knit or sew to keep my mind occupied; on the fine days, I'd go out.

I was getting good at it, too. When I started catching the buses first, Scott would ride along with me until I got used to bus numbers, routes, and transfers. He'd spend hours after school and on weekends doing the same common routes over and over. Scott was good to me. For a teenaged boy to be hanging out with his grandmother and without complaint, he had to be a good young fellow. Wherever I wanted to go, he'd show me how to get there and make sure I knew it before he'd let me go on my own.

After a few months at Mary's, I got into a routine that I planned not to let become a rut. I'd get up and make breakfast for myself. Once I cleaned the dishes and got dressed, it would be going on ten o'clock. Most days I'd go to the Avalon Mall. I'd sit in the food court and drink coffee. People would come and go, and I even made "mall friends," strangers, mostly seniors, who did the same as me, got out of the house while they were able. Some days I'd go to the Village Mall, but for the most part, I centred around the Avalon Mall.

People from North Harbour often looked for me there once I started going regularly. We'd have coffee and catch up. If there was nobody around, I'd people-watch. It was a great pastime.

Sometimes, I'd get brave or bored or both. One day, I had to return a purchase at the Village. Mary and I had been in there the weekend before, and I'd bought something that I no longer wanted. I did the return and checked the bus schedule so I could be at the main entrance when the buses came. On the half-hour, there was usually a dozen or so lined up outside so that they could align transfers from one to the other. They weren't in any order, so I had to be careful to catch the correct one.

This particular morning, the sun was shining directly behind the buses and making it hard to see the number. I walked out of the Village and crossed the street. As I was going toward the first bus, I looked up for the number I wanted, but with the sun in my eyes, I couldn't tell one from the other. The glare was blinding me.

I went a little farther and didn't know a thing until I hit the cement sidewalk. Blood gushed from my face, and I became disoriented for the moment. Before I knew what was happening, a bus driver and passenger picked me up, brought me on board, and sat me in the front seat.

The only phone number I could think of in that moment was Ida's cell. The bus driver called her and told her I'd fallen but that I was all right. She was working nearby and told the driver she was on her way.

Two passengers got off and returned with paper towels to stop the bleeding, the driver called the terminal to say he'd be delayed, and they sat with me and waited and tended to my face. I was tormented about causing the bus to be stopped for so long, but the driver wasn't concerned and said not to let it bother me.

Ida showed up about ten minutes later and took me to the hospital. My nose wasn't broken, but I had to get several stitches where my eyeglasses had cut through the skin. I had two black eyes after that.

But neither the black eyes nor the stitches kept me fastened to the house. If I stayed in then, I would find it hard to go out again. So, though I was fearful of a misstep, I caught the bus and went to the Avalon Mall the next day. I became extra careful after that so that I wouldn't give myself a legacy like the broken leg from years before.

I became more confident and wasn't afraid to tackle anything. After going to Florida with May a few times, I started flying places on my own. In July 2007, Eddy wanted me to go to Ontario for a few weeks, and so I decided to take him up on the offer. It was the first time travelling alone, and I was almost seventy-four. I stayed with Eddy for a month, with a few nights at Larry and Caroline's in between.

Neil and Trudy had moved to Thompson, Manitoba, from Edmonton, and I hadn't seen them in over a year. I flew from Ontario to Winnipeg to meet up with them, and we drove north to Thompson. I was only planning to stay for a few weeks or a month, but they wanted me to stay longer. I had plans to come home in November at first and then thought of them having nobody around for Christmas, so I stayed on, ringing in the New Year in Manitoba. It would be March before I decided to go home, with another stop in Ontario on the way.

In St. John's, I got back into the mall routine. But old habits and the need to be useful were a strong calling within me. The nightly visits to my parents, the care for my mother, the care for Eddy, and staying with May in the winters were things that, though hard on times, gave me a sense of fulfillment and purpose. All that was involved was giving time. Though I enjoyed the travel and seeing something new, I wanted to be useful. Time was something I had lots of now.

Over the years, Aunt Annie's daughter, my cousin Ida (now Bennett) was a person I'd admired. She'd been knocking at death's door on more than one occasion, and she still greeted the world with a smile. Ida had had many surgeries over the past number of years and would often joke that she had more parts missing than she had attached. I often marvelled at her good-natured attitude despite her infirmities.

When she lived in Mount Carmel, and after Eddy died, several times I'd get somebody to drive me over and stay with Ida for the night. She had home care and had family around her, but I liked to spend time with her. We'd play cards and laugh and talk well into the night. I genuinely enjoyed her company.

We also had a kinship of sorts. Being widows and losing children, that though we didn't speak about, was a common, invisible thread that linked us. Bonds of understanding and comradeship like ours many are fortunate not to know.

After several health setbacks, Ida ended up at St. Patrick's Mercy Home—St. Pat's, as it was commonly known—in St. John's. Visiting Ida was something I could easily do, and so my ritual began. After spending an hour or so at the Avalon Mall, I'd catch the bus as far as Elizabeth Avenue to St. Pat's.

On rainy days, if there was a big shower, or if it was cold and windy, the driver would let me off right in front of the home. The drivers knew me by now and looked out for me.

Ida looked forward to my visit every day and had the cards ready. If any of her children were visiting, she'd tell them to go on, she wanted to play cards with me. They'd laugh at how I was more important than them, and she'd agree, her shaking laughter so much like my own mother's and her namesake. Ida's family began to time their visits so as not to interfere with "Catherine's time."

Such a wonderful soul as Ida was hard to come by. We'd play cards for a few hours until it was time for me to catch the bus home. She didn't want to see me go, and I hated leaving her, but she knew I'd be back the next day. If I wouldn't be able to come see her because I was going somewhere or I had an appointment or something, she'd be disappointed but never made me feel like I *had* to visit her. I really enjoyed our time together.

In 2010, May's son Cecil asked his mother and me to meet him in Halifax, spend a few days with his sister, and accompany him on the drive home. May kept at me to go, as she didn't want to travel on her own, so I said yes. I told Ida I was going, and she was happy and sad at the same time. There had been a change in her of late, and she was struggling to talk. Even sitting up to play cards was hard on her, but she did it, anyway. I promised I'd be up to see her as soon as I got back. She was delighted with that.

Not long after we left, Ida became sicker, and it was questionable whether she'd survive. We were only in Nova Scotia a day when we learned that Ida had died. Cecil knew how much she meant to me, so he changed the reservation for the ferry. We cut our visit short and headed home. We were expected to get back on the day of her funeral. I wanted to see Ida and was worried we wouldn't make it. But her family delayed the funeral for me, knowing I was on my way. I was comforted in my chance to say goodbye to my dear cousin and friend.

I learned a lot about perseverance from Ida Bennett.

27

The Breath of Life

I noticed a few times, as I climbed the hill from the bus stop to St. Pat's main doors to visit Ida Bennett, I'd be near to gasping for air. At first I thought it was caused by the muggy weather or not enough walking. It only happened a few times, and I didn't really give it much attention. I took a break or two to catch my breath and then moved on. As with anything you see through a backward lens, those few episodes were probably the beginning of the next mountain that was put before me.

I continued my daily trek to the mall, confident in my abilities to manage the buses. On the way back to Mary's, I'd take the shortcut between the houses on Newfoundland Drive and come out at the top of the steps across the road from Mary's townhouse.

As the days rolled into months, I found myself, only on some days, having difficulty on the few steps between the bus and Mary's. I blamed my age and my dependence on the bus instead of my two legs as the reason. I resolved to do more walking to see if it would help. I didn't want to lose my independence after only recently finding it.

With winter coming, I spent more time "mall walking" to stay fit. I enjoyed the roaming and the company. As part of the routine, Clyde Bennett, Ida's son, met me there almost every day. We'd laugh and talk and spend hours in the food court with a cup of coffee. When Clyde was away working, there would be others that took his place. I rarely spent a lunchtime by myself in the mall. I couldn't help but think that maybe they were doing for me what I'd been doing for Ida.

Staying with May also became the routine during the winters. In 2009, at the height of the H1N1 scare, I came down with what I called the flu. I wasn't tested for the virus, but I had all the symptoms despite having had the flu shot. I became terribly sick for almost two weeks. I could hardly lift my head from the pillow, and in the end, I contracted pneumonia.

This took the good out of me, and I don't believe I ever fully recovered after that. I became short-breathed more often and lacked energy to do the simplest things. When I returned to the mall, I found myself having to take several rests between the bus and the intermission. There were days I couldn't do it at all and stayed home at Mary's.

I knew there was something wrong. There was a heaviness in my chest. I had test after test and was finally sent to see a lung specialist to figure out the underlying cause of my weakness. More tests, and I was put on oxygen for the times when I was walking.

This helped a bit, and I was able to get back more often to my daily routine. When I got the canisters of oxygen, I figured I'd be chained to the house and that Mary would have to help me change tanks. But after some time and practice, I was able to do it for myself. That gave me a bit more freedom, and despite the need to carry the oxygen around, I was glad to get out.

But whatever I had progressed, and full-time oxygen was required. The lung specialist said he couldn't figure out what disease or condition I had; it wasn't something he had seen before. He reached out across the country for something similar, but nothing. So, for the sake of naming it, he said he'd say I had pulmonary hypertension, a high blood pressure in the lungs, even though I didn't fully fit that mould. My disease was unique in many respects.

So, the way forward was being chained to canisters if I wanted to go out. That meant I either had to carry a tank while walking, or, if I was in a car, I could take as many as I needed. A tank wasn't light, nor was it small. We tried to get a portable machine, but I didn't qualify. I had one for home use, which plugged in, and I had a long plastic line that let me move about the house.

At Mary's, I limited my trips to the bathroom, which was upstairs, because to get there I was at the point that I needed to crawl. The exertion was too much for me. It was the same for my bedroom; that, too, was upstairs. Struggling up the stairs became too much.

My freedom was gone. On the weekends, Mary or one of the others would come for me and take me for a drive. I loved driving, because I was moving, and moving was something I missed. I got a walker to carry the oxygen and went to the mall every now and again, though accompanied by somebody instead of independently. The buses were over at this point. I missed May's company in the winter. I was heartbroken when she passed away in March 2013. I spent two days at the hospital in her final days and was comforted in being with her and my nieces and nephews when she died.

As my health declined and my ability to move about Mary's place became more limited, Ida asked me to come out and live with her. She had a houseful but had a room for me where the bathroom and bedroom were on the one level. We packed up all my belongings, and I started over again, this time in Conception Bay South.

Ida travelled a lot for work, and in the beginning, her husband, Thomas, worked in Alberta. He'd be gone for two-thirds of the month and back for seven or eight days. When the two of them were gone, I went to Mary's or Neil and Trudy's. But when it got harder to go, and with trying to pack enough oxygen, either Mary or Trudy came and stayed with me.

When I turned eighty, the family had a big party for me in the community hall in North Harbour. People I hadn't seen in years came; nearly everyone in the place came along as well. It was a wonderful night with lots of reminiscing. My most precious gift was a memory box where people sent notes about how we were connected.

Eddy wanted me to go to Toronto for a week and bought me a ticket. So, with Mary as my support, we left the day after the party. Never one not to be in a tangle of some sort, the flight we were on had their own oxygen and wouldn't use mine. Eddy arranged for canisters and the plug-in system, hoses, and everything that I needed for when we got there.

Larry and Caroline were supposed to pick us up and brought a canister early to allow me to transfer from the plane's oxygen when we arrived. Because I needed help, I had to wait until last to get off the plane.

All went well until it didn't. When the stewardess brought the oxygen, took me off the plane's supply, and hooked me up, the canister was empty. She put me back on the plane's oxygen, and Mary got off and contacted Larry. I wasn't allowed to deplane, as I was in their care.

Larry said they'd just picked up the oxygen supply and that they had more in the car. Both he and Caroline left the arrivals area to get another canister. Unfortunately, they went to the wrong level at the parking garage and couldn't find the car. Then they couldn't remember where they parked, and at the Toronto Pearson Airport, that was a huge problem.

While I waited, the cleanup crew came aboard after asking if I minded. Of course, I didn't. I was getting fidgety and tormented by then. Mary wasn't allowed to get back on, either. The cleaners finished, and I still waited. I had no way of knowing what was going on outside. Then I started imagining all the things that could have gone wrong and that nobody would tell me.

The captain got aboard for the next flight, and the crew spoke about being late. The stewardess continued to check on me, because the oxygen tank they had on board was getting empty. They only had enough for the trip with a little to spare. After more than thirty minutes, the tank ran out. The girl was frantic as she moved me from the seat into a wheelchair.

Though I told her I'd be all right, she quickly pushed me up the passenger boarding bridge.

When we got off the ramp and into the airport, there were lineups waiting to board, and I was sure every eye was turned to me. Though I doubt that was true, it was how I felt. Mary stood to the side, on the phone, trying to find out what happened to Larry and Caroline. They had just then handed off the canister to a waiting attendant in the arrivals area, and that would take five minutes to get to us.

The stewardess told Mary to follow her, and she booted it toward the incoming canister, fearful of what my being without the oxygen support would mean. We met somewhere in the middle and quickly set me up. By this time, I was struggling to breathe. But I was more tormented about delaying the plane and everything else that I had no control over but tortured me, anyway. That day, I swore it would be my last trip anywhere that I couldn't get back from on the same day. Travelling had become too complex.

However, I would go once more. Cecil had been planning on taking his mother and me to the Shrine of Sainte-Anne-de-Beaupré in Quebec. When his mother died, he still wanted me to go with him. In his mother's place, he took Marg. He made all the arrangements for a few days at the Shrine and, thankfully, everything went smoothly. That was my last trip aboard an airplane.

28

Another False Start

I had been in and out of the hospital and no closer to feeling better. I had very little use in my legs, and my breathing wasn't helped by the oxygen. I joined a heart monitoring program put in place by Eastern Health. Ida took my blood pressure, weight, and oxygen levels every day. She recorded the results on an iPad, which were fed through a program whereby I'd get a call if adjustments were needed in medication. After graduating from this program, I had no other means of being monitored except to go to the hospital.

My pulse often dropped into the twenties. To get to the bathroom was a struggle. I tried to go as little as possible because there was nobody home. I didn't know if I could get back. Ida would get a lunch ready for me before she went to work, but I often couldn't get out to even get something to eat.

After being in the emergency room all night on Boxing Night in 2016, I had several litres of fluid taken off, and my breathing got better for about three weeks. My legs were still heavy, though, and I couldn't get up out of the chair. When Ida got home from work a week later and saw that I couldn't make my way to the bathroom, she bundled me up and we went back again.

This time I had a chest X-ray, and after ten minutes, the ER doctor told me I was old and sick and dying. He said that I should go home; there was nothing to be done for me. We were in a bit of shock at what was said, because I thought this was it. The doctor should know. I'd go back to Ida's, get in the chair, and die. I wasn't sure how long we'd have to wait or anything, but it seemed so final.

Ida was mad. On the way home, she told me she was going to report the doctor. I asked her not to, but she didn't listen to me.

The next morning, Ida took me to my family doctor, and he prescribed antibiotics and gave me a slip for bloodwork. The following day, I started to feel a little better. That same day, a doctor from the ER called and told Ida that my X-ray had been reviewed and I had fluid on my lungs. The doctor said that Ida could take me back in and be seen as a priority if she wanted. She asked me what I wanted to do, but I was feeling a bit better, so I said no. It was too difficult to be getting in and out of vehicles, and I believed the antibiotics would work. Ida got a nurse to come in and do my bloodwork.

Though the antibiotics perked me up for a few weeks, I began feeling miserable once they were gone. I had a scheduled appointment with my respirologist a week later, so I decided I would wait. After an exam, he looked at me and told me to go to the ER. Ida wheeled me up, and we sat there for several hours. I could barely hold up my head. Some people saw how sick I was and offered to give me their place in line, but I couldn't get in. Ida checked with the desk every thirty minutes and called my respiratory doctor. He called back, but I still couldn't get in.

Neil and Trudy came and waited with us. I ran out of oxygen and had to get the hospital staff to hook up a tank for me. Finally, after almost seven hours in the waiting room, the people changed at the desk, and one clerk took pity on me and sent me to fast track.

I got called in by a nice lady doctor who listened to my heart and looked at my chart. When she saw the check-in time, she asked Ida why I had been out in the waiting room so long. She looked at bloodwork that the family doctor had ordered the week before and told me that I had no blood.

She ordered a stretcher for me and said I had to go to the other side of the ER.

"Do we have to wait again?" I asked. I didn't know how much longer I could wait. I was tired.

"No, I'll send you there from here," she said as she patted my hand.

Ida asked who the doctor was over there and found out it was the same fellow who had told me to go home and die the last time I'd been there. She explained what happened to the fast track doctor.

The doctor looked at me. "Is that true?" Her eyes were wide with disbelief, as if she was in shock that a colleague would have said it.

"Yes, he told me I was old and dying, that I should go home." I nodded as I said it.

She took my hands, closed her eyes, and hung her head. When she looked up at me, her eyes were watering. She grabbed a tissue, then fiddled with the papers on her lap before she took my hands again. "I'm sorry that happened to you. I don't understand how somebody could say that."

"It wasn't you," I said.

"I hope it never is," she said as she got up and opened the door to let in the stretcher.

"I am here until 2:00 a.m., and I will monitor you on the other side. You won't have to see any other doctor."

"I don't want him to know I told what he said."

"He won't know," she said. "I assure you that you will be under my care over there."

I was kept in the ER for two days and given three bags of blood. It was easier to breathe after that. At least for a little while. A month later, I was back in for more. This time, I had an iron infusion as well. I had all kinds of tests and was getting sick of being poked and prodded with no better outcome than the time before.

Finally, after umpteen trips to the hospital and multiple stays, a cardiologist took me on. My medication was upped from 20 mg to 120 mg, and I lost almost thirty pounds of fluid weight over the week in the hospital. I was assigned a social worker, and he recommended that I either get home care or go to a place where I wouldn't be alone during the days.

I thought back to the time that Jer was in the home and how he cried for somebody to take him out, and I didn't want to go to a place like that. I didn't want strangers at Ida's, either. But Ida was adamant that I be monitored, because we didn't know how long I'd be okay. She got approval for somebody to come and get meals for me.

Several girls came to the house over the next month. I was tormented about it. People were there when Ida and Thomas were home. Some days I didn't know who was coming, and sometimes nobody showed up.

Ida was worried about me and mentioned to me again about going to a retirement home. I didn't want to hear tell of it. But with her travelling so much, it was too hard to be coming and going out to here or there for a week or having somebody come and stay with me, so I went to Neil and Trudy's for a while. I was only there ten days when I got sick again and ended up back in the hospital. This time, I needed more blood and platelets.

I could no longer be without care, according to the social worker. The writing was before me. I had to go to a seniors home. He prepared the papers. Because I was now considered urgent care, I'd have to go from the hospital to the first available bed. That could be anywhere in the coverage area, according to the rules. A couple of places came up as available but were hours away from everyone.

Admittedly, I was mad, but I couldn't say anything. But more certainly, I was closer to scared. I knew this was going to be the way of it from then on, and I had absolutely no control over anything regarding my life. The fact was I was homeless and had been for a long time. Being truthful with myself, it was probably since June 19, 1980.

Ida wouldn't let me go so far away, so we decided on more home care at her place to tide me over until a spot became available close by. Ida ended up in surgery to have her gallbladder removed and developed a hernia shortly after. She was unable to provide any assistance to me in getting up or going around the house. The last thing I wanted was Ida hurting herself. I knew there was no choice now, and it was a waiting game.

My saving grace in all of it was Marg. She faithfully called me every night at nine. We struck up that tradition long before I'd left North Harbour and after Eddy had gotten sick. I was sure Marg would raise the spirits of the dead if there were such a thing. She was the highlight of many of my days. We talked about going to a home and what it meant for me. Marg listened to my fears and helped calm them.

29

Decades of the Rosary

Growing up, reciting the rosary daily was commonplace in every household in North Harbour. The rosary has seasons; back then, there were three. The five Joyful Mysteries were said the most, the five Sorrowful Mysteries during Lent, and the Glorious Mysteries during Easter.

As a young girl, I liked to go to my uncle Jack's during the rosary. Admittedly, it wasn't for prayer but for fun. More so, making fun. Both my friend Mary and I would often skip in the lane to Uncle Jack and Aunt Rose's around six o'clock, knowing full well they'd be just kneeling down for prayer.

The rosary would be different there. Aunt Rose would start and then remember something she was going to ask my uncle, and they'd have a short conversation between the Hail Mary and the Holy Mary or wherever the thought struck her.

We'd titter, Aunt Rose would tell us to knock it off, and Uncle Jack would give us a stern look. We'd stop for the moment, and when they were back in prayer, one of us would nudge the other and shake and hold back the snickers when their backs were to us. We'd be holy and prayerful when they were looking our way.

My father's God had been the sea and my mother, and my mother's God in turn was my father and the harbour. Though I was no stranger to the rosary, daily recitation wasn't as prevalent to me at home.

When I married Eddy, we'd say the rosary every evening after supper. If Eddy was home, the rosary was said, and whoever showed up would kneel the same as if they were home.

When Mary was little, I'd put her to bed and then it was time for the rosary. One particular evening, Albert Linehan and Dave Dalton came in just before we started. Halfway through the second or third Mystery, Mary started to cry, which soon turned into a howl. I got up and ran up the stairs while Eddy took over the Hail Mary part that I was saying, and the others continued to answer with the Holy Mary.

When I got Mary settled and came down over the stairs, all hands were laughing and snickering. They tried to stop when they saw me coming. I looked at Eddy, and he burst out laughing.

I scowled my displeasure at the shenanigans. "What happened to the rosary?"

"We finished the Mystery and were trying to think of the next one," Albert piped up.

"I knew it was something in the Temple," Dave said, grinning.

"So, what happened?" I asked, trying to understand what was going on.

"Eddy said a smack in the temple," Albert said, and they all burst out laughing once again.

I turned the two of them out, then, because I knew we'd never get to finish it if they were there. They went on but were back, chuckling and grinning, the following evening, not at all put out at having to leave the evening before.

When we moved to North Harbour, it was common, again, to say the rosary after supper. Since we had ten children, we settled on saying two, one Mystery for each child. Everyone would stop what they were doing and kneel around together, bent over chair seats, or on chairs or the bench bent over the table. Once they were old enough, each one would take a Mystery in their turn.

After the fire, Eddy continued in this tradition. He'd kneel for the rosary every evening after supper. I'd had my fill of the rosary then and wouldn't say it. He'd never ask me to join him, and I'd walk around doing dishes or simply avoided him while doing insignificant chores. Sometimes I'd even leave and go down the road to see my parents.

Eddy started reciting the prayers earlier then, sometimes around one o'clock. I kept clear and ignored the gnawing feeling that I was wrong in doing what I was doing. I guess I was mad with God for my devotion to the rosary over the years and what it had gotten me. But Eddy didn't falter. He also went to the church every single day no matter the weather since we moved to North Harbour, and he continued both the rosary and the church visit after the fire.

It would be months before I'd kneel in prayer. But I missed it. So, one day, Eddy was leaning in across the table, ready to start, and I pulled a pillow from the daybed and bent in on the other side of the table with the cushion under my knees.

I believe this was the beginning of my healing the rift I had with God.

We moved the recital back to after supper and continued the tradition. Whenever any of the children were around, they'd sometimes join or sometimes go on about their business while we prayed the rosary.

After Eddy died, the rosary became my private time. I'd take my beads to bed and pray before I went to sleep. If there was somebody sick or asked me for prayers, I'd say it several times a day when I was by myself. The rosary became a companion, keeping me company in the passing of time.

Though I had a reprieve after the last hospital stay because I got a little bit better, I was able to go to Ida's while I waited for a place to open up for me nearby. I was lucky in many regards, though I didn't feel lucky at the time. Now the clock ticked in my head, a countdown of sorts, to the time a space opened at the personal care home.

I began to pray the rosary for myself. This time, they were pleas for acceptance. I didn't ask for health of body but health of mind, to bear the separation from family and the thoughts of being somehow abandoned by everyone to the care of strangers.

When word came that a spot was available, I knew that was it. I prayed and prayed. It consumed me. I found my anger at the situation changed and softened without me knowing it. Ida packed up my stuff. We were all quiet. Although I knew it was hard on her, I also prayed there'd be another way.

As the date loomed, February 28, 2018, my mind was tossed. I reluctantly accepted I was going, and I prayed the rosary on autopilot that I'd be all right with it. Ida went through my clothes with me. They had to be marked with the room number so my shirts and pants wouldn't be mixed up with others. For a fleeting moment I thought that's what they probably did in prison, too.

On the day I was moving, Mary came out for me to take me to the home. I thought I'd be afraid that day, but I wasn't. I felt the same as if we were going to the mall or to a restaurant.

That day, I walked into Admirals Coast Retirement Centre and into a new life.

Mary helped get me settled away that first day. Staff came in and introduced themselves. I was shown my place in the dining area, given some material to read, and had my picture taken to put on the door. I was in a room with another lady; she had the window. That night, I prayed to be accepting of my new residence.

Ida, Mary, and Trudy came every day and helped put up pictures and took me on tours of the various wings of the building. I told them that nobody needed to be with me all the time, that I was all right, but they came anyway. After about a week, I was getting to know the residents and staff and realized that I didn't need to pray the rosary for myself, because I simply liked the place.

I left my room and found a card game that needed one more person. I sat in and started a nightly ritual. People dropped by my room and welcomed me. I realized that there was an enormous divide between what I thought the place would be like and what it was actually like. Things had changed a lot from the time I'd picked up Jer at the home in Holyrood to today. I believe that notion had made me warier than necessary.

When Ida came in, I told her I wished I had gone there sooner. I wasn't just saying it. I meant it. She had such a look of relief on her face, it made me smile.

"I didn't know what I would have done if you hated it," she said.

"I prayed about it."

"So did I," she said. "I cried about it, too."

"I knew you couldn't bring me up here, because you'd be crying."

"As soon as you went through the door, I started," Ida said with a grin and water-soaked eyes. "I cried for days."

"I'm the best kind here. I thought it would be different. But I like it," I said again. "I should have been here sooner."

I could see her expression soften. She reached for my hand, tears spilled over, and she hugged me.

"I really don't know what I would have done if you hated it," she said. "But I would have done something."

I took myself off my prayer list. I was all right.

30

A Never-Ending Story

At Admirals Coast Retirement Centre, I settled into a routine. I had lots of friends and activities to keep me busy. The children and grandchildren and great-grandchildren came to visit as well as friends and other family members. I liked it there.

My first month, the oxygen canisters ran out because I was using them while out playing cards and to go to all my meals in the dining room. Meals were served to my room for a few days, and though I missed chatting with other residents at the tables, I missed the camaraderie of the card games most of all.

The monthly supply of oxygen was delivered, and I was back in business again. When it happened at the end of the second month, I told Ida and Mary about it. Ida bought an extra tank and had it added to my supply. That still didn't quite reach to the end of thirty-one days.

"Apparently, you are only supposed to breathe for twenty-eight days," Ida said when she brought in another tank to me. "I'm not sure what you are supposed to do on the longer months."

"I'm all right. I don't mind," I told her.

"It's not the point, Mom," she said. "For seniors in homes, it is isolating enough. No need to make it worse. I'm on the case, though. You'll be assessed for one of those portable machines in a few days."

"I thought I didn't qualify," I said.

"You didn't until I went back there this time," Ida said. "It wasn't easy to make them understand that you keep running out. But after four visits there and a word with the manager, they see it now."

Ida laughed. I was sure she'd had more than a word with the manager, but I wouldn't ask.

A few days later, I got a battery-charged oxygen pack and, for a little while, at least, freedom. Now I didn't have to worry about sparing my oxygen along. I had it when I needed it. I got used to putting it on and taking it off the charger in no time. It was easier to carry than the canisters. Now my oxygen shortage worries were settled.

Mary, who had retired by now, took me out for drives, sometimes to North Harbour, where I could visit with Marg and Dick as well as Neil and Trudy.

I was worried about Marg. Though she called me every night to see how I was doing, when I'd ask her, she'd simply say, "I'm all right." I knew she wasn't.

When Marg went into palliative care a few weeks after I'd seen her last, I couldn't believe it. Ida brought me out. I could barely get along the corridor with my walker. The closer I got to her room, the harder it was to breathe. I cried when I saw her lying there. I sat, held her hand, and prayed. It was unbelievable, and I couldn't imagine how Dick and her sons and daughters felt. To me, it didn't feel real. It was too out of sorts with how things, in my mind, were supposed to be.

Marg and I often kidded around about who'd be gone first. That sounds morbid, but it's true. I thought, with everything that was wrong with me, I'd be well cold before Marg would come. I could even imagine her out in the home with me, playing cards, laughing, and talking. Marg would have quickly adjusted and probably ask to go there, because that was how she was. She had foresight and wisdom and courage for as long as I knew her.

Saying goodbye that day, I told her I loved her. There was nothing else to say. The struggle to leave was more difficult than the struggle to get there. The crush of what was to come would be mighty.

I was right. Aside from the youngsters, Marg's death hit me the hardest of any. Her words from the few weeks before resonated with me. "If I go to the doctor tomorrow and I'm all right, then I'll be all right. If I'm not all right, then I'll be all right, anyway."

That was Marg, plunging forward, unafraid. Such was her faith and her trust in whatever is beyond this. Thoughts of Marg and her absence brought a freshness to the absence of others no longer in my life. Her friendship was one I'll never forget and be more than grateful for as long as my days draw out.

It wasn't long after that that Susie Feaver came to Admirals Coast. I believed it was Marg who sent her, because she reminded me so much of my dearest friend. Susie was a constant, a best friend. As a former nurse, she had a kind and caring way about her that drew me to her in a special bond.

A few months after Suzie came, I began to falter once again. I found it hard to get to the dining room. The distance caused me to gasp for breath, and a few times I believed the mobile oxygen unit wasn't working. It was tested and okay, so something else had to be going on.

After a few trips to the hospital and more doctors' appointments, I found out it was my heart that was causing the new trouble. As one thing got fixed, another popped up. I was scheduled to have a pacemaker put in. That was a hard procedure. I felt the pressure of it for days. In the end, having the pacemaker gave me a better quality of life. At least for a little while.

My body began to drag again a few months later. This time, I was admitted to the Health Sciences Centre, as my blood count numbers were half what they should be. After testing, there was no way to figure out where it was going. I got topped up and sent back to Admirals Coast to recuperate.

Recuperation was not to be. I ended up back in emergency in the Health Sciences Centre for seven days. I received more blood, but in the end, I'd start over once again. This time, I was sent to a higher level of care facility because my legs had given out. After three months of physical therapy and setbacks, Pleasantview Towers became my new start-over place.

My eyes have become waterier as my body deteriorates toward its end. The will to be strong in facing the health challenges that seem constant now is not as solid as it once was. That, too, has quickly declined in the last few years. As I face one thing after another after another, I sometimes wonder what it's all about. I guess I'll know soon enough, when the time is right. Being locked away from family because of the pandemic is the hardest.

I'll have to start over one more time. According to the things I've believed all my life, it will be either heaven or hell. My preference is the first one, because I think I've been living the second one for as long as I can remember and for long enough. But I don't get the final say in that.

I don't say this to be pitied but to be understood. My life is what it is and has been what it has been. It isn't a fairy tale, nor has it been easy. But I laughed when I could and enjoyed what I could. I don't compare my life to that of others, because that would be fruitless. There are lots of people who have fared worse off than I have. I only know I did the best I could and the best I knew how with what was put before me.

CONCLUSION

From the Author:
Forty Years of Fire Days

Global pandemic restrictions meant we had to cancel the forty-year memorial service planned for June 19, 2020. It also meant there were limitations on what we could do for Mom. I was not only her designated visitor at Admirals Coast Retirement Centre but also the person living the closest. Like the others, I was able to see her through her room window and talk via phone when her roommate, who slept by the window, was gone for several weeks. I also video-chatted with her. That was with the help of the recreation director, one day a week.

June is typically a hard month on Mom. She thinks about what happened more, and it plays on her mind. But with COVID-19, it was a sadder and lonelier time for her. The staff and her friends in the residence did all they could for her, but her eyes held no light nor life, she didn't chat, and each June seemed to be worse than the last. With nobody around, she was as close to despondent as I'd ever seen her.

When restrictions lifted, she was overjoyed to know somebody was finally allowed in and could get close without barriers. Because of proximity, it was easiest for me to go. I brought technology that connected her to everyone. She got to talk over video to family and friends, not just once per week but as often as I could get to see her.

However, "Fire Day" is always "Fire Day," no matter what, and she was deeply troubled that it would be the first time she didn't go home to "see the young ones."

I contacted Admirals Coast administration to see if there was any way in the world to make it happen. At that time, she was only allowed to be taken out for an appointment, so I made one up. I suppose I shouldn't admit that there was nothing scheduled for her, but here it is. I believed the day was extraordinary enough that I'd be forgiven if found out. I also booked the day off work. Work was from home, and I made sure I was not in contact with anyone, nor did I go out leading up to the "Fire Day."

Her nephew, Father Cecil Critch, said a memorial Mass at 9:00 a.m. on Friday, June 19, at the Basilica of St. John the Baptist in St. John's. As it was televised, I arranged with staff to have the Mass streamed to Admirals Coast in the common room. More than half the residents showed up to support her that morning.

I was gloved and masked and sanitized and stayed in the corner as it was being played. I was emotional and was glad to be at the back of the room, where nobody could see me gulp and swallow hard or blink to hold back the threatening tears.

She sat alone, with chairs more than three feet on either side of her, as she watched the screen. Seeing her there, by herself, without comfort, was miles beyond sad. It reminded me that that must have been how she felt on the day of the fire.

Alone.

I couldn't carry her sorrow. No one could. And she carried it with grace today.

At the end of Mass, she remained seated while the others left, passing before her, reaching for her hand, trying to comfort her. I had no idea how many of them were reliving their own terrible sufferings, how many had lost a child, nor how many knew the pain she carried.

Once the area had cleared, I went to her.

"That was a lovely service," she said.

"It was beautiful." I nodded and smiled solemnly beneath the mask, hoping she could see it in my eyes.

"You know I don't know one thing that he said, don't you?"

I nodded. "Cecil named all five of them, and Dad, too," I said. I struggled for air as I tried to keep my emotions from overflowing. "He asked everyone to pray for you and all the residents here at Admirals Coast."

"That was nice of him." She looked up at me then, her eyes glistening. "Though I didn't hear it, I loved it. That might not make sense, but I did love it."

"It makes sense to me."

I braced to pull her from the chair. She pushed her walker to her room. Each step was laborious. I retrieved her coat and purse, and we made our way to the door. She was silent. So was I.

We didn't speak much as we drove the hour to North Harbour. I wanted to let her take the lead, and perhaps, admittedly, I couldn't talk myself, either.

I pulled up in the cemetery, past the gate, and as close to the graves as I could get. There was a marshy area between the lane and the gravesite, and the sod was uneven. It was a greyish day with brooding skies as we were driving, or perhaps it was the atmosphere in the car. But when we arrived in North Harbour, the sky was clear and the sun shone, reminding me of the morning of the fire.

Forty years between that day and this one. "Impossible" came to mind, yet here it was.

Mom's breathing was particularly heavy, and her knee had given out months before, making it difficult to get around.

"You're as close as I can get you," I said as I moved around the car to help her get out. The laneway was very narrow, and a few bigger rocks on the side kept the area from falling into the marshy spot. The solid layer was barely more than the width of the car.

"I'm going over," she said. "I don't care if it kills me." She struggled to pull her legs out and then slid to the ground, bracing herself on the door handle and the seat back. I grabbed her oxygen tank, and we sidled along the car until we could safely step down to the wet ground. Then, we had to make our way over to the graves.

I recalled the day that I had come back to North Harbour months after the fire and visited here for the first time. Mom and I had gone to the graveyard, and we linked arms across this forty-foot expanse that could as well have been like trying to reach the horizon. With each step she took back then, she was pushing closer to the ground while trying to bear me up at the same time. I had been so weak, and she was heavy on me both physically and emotionally. She had barely made it that day. Today was similar, but I was stronger. She struggled on the wet ground, she couldn't lift her leg high enough to get over the humps and hollows, and each step was an indrawn breath of pain. I knew it wasn't just physical.

We took two breaks going the short distance. Her eyes fixated on the destination with anticipation and dread. Her breath was coming in shallow gasps. She was determined.

It took about ten minutes to reach the bench that overlooked the plot. Neil had mowed, and everything was tidy. I helped her down onto the seat and sat with her for a few moments.

"I can't believe what happened here," she said. "How could this happen? How could this happen to us?"

She wasn't expecting a response, but I whispered, "I don't know, Mom."

I held her hand, and we sat in silence. She looked from one black stone to the other and the other. Her head stopped at each one while memories crossed the years. More vivid today because of the date.

Bees buzzed, birds chirped, the sun shone bright, and a tiny breeze kissed our faces for a mere moment. She reached to her brow and closed her eyes.

"I still can't believe it, sometimes," she said, her voice so low I thought she was talking to herself. I know their presence is eternally missed. She doesn't have to say it. They are the absence of light. Like shadows bruising where the sun cannot see, though the picture is bright on the canvas. Every second, every minute, every hour has that shadow. It moves and darkens and lightens but is there. The absence of five lives that she bore while the weight of motherhood remains, the weight of love for what is missing. The load is tremendous on this day.

I left her there, then. I wanted her to have time by herself to pray. I watched her from a few feet behind. Her feebleness was amplified by an internal pain that, in that moment, also strengthened her. The forty years were gone. The wounds were fresh and raw. The memories were vivid. This was her time with her loss, her time with her pain. They couldn't be spoken back to life, but I'm sure today memories brought her as close as she could come.

My own memories came, strong and bitter and beautiful. The sun beat down on us as if to somehow ease that which cannot be relieved.

I took pictures of her, of the graves, of the surrounding trees, and of the ocean so I could share with family. The pandemic had taken away our ability to gather, and everyone who could would have been with her today.

Wandering around the nearby graves, I watched until her shoulders dipped just a little lower. So, I sat with her again. She leaned on me, and I prayed for her. Forty years had been hard on us all, but my mother bore the most. I was a sister in it; she was a mother. Thinking of my own children, I was presented with the "un" words—unbearable, unbelievable, unthinkable—that I was so grateful not to know as a mother or a grandmother. She was not as fortunate.

I thought of her waning strength in a body that was betraying her, but her fortitude and will to continue on, to get up every morning, was there so she could be tough for us all. Her mothering to us was never lessened. It wasn't cut in half. It deepened.

I took in the massive spruce a few feet from us. That was her, strong, and despite its worn and weathered raggedness, broken limbs, and rinding trunk, it was beautiful to behold. It stood guard here in this sacred place. I couldn't help but acknowledge that it waited for us and would be there after we were gone.

Reaching my hand to pat hers, we strengthened each other. The touch was not to comfort what couldn't be comforted but to share. I pulled her up when the time was right, and she fumbled back to the car.

"I can't go without seeing Marg," she said. "I'd never have gotten through it without her."

"Marg it is, my dear," I said.

We drove up around to the top of the graveyard. She rolled down her window and reached out as if Marg was waiting for her trembling hand. A slight breeze tousled her hair. Perhaps she was.

"Marg was my dearest friend. I certainly miss her. I never thought she'd be gone ahead of me." Her voice faltered, and tears rose and glistened in her eyes.

"She was a great friend." I missed her, too.

I drove down through the harbour so she could see the changes from the last time she'd been there. We stopped by Jos's and said hello from the car to the step. We'd been there forty years prior, too. We didn't say what day it was. Jos knew.

I bought Mom fish and chips at the restaurant on the return trip. We ate in the car. She talked about the day of the fire, the things she heard, the things she saw, and the things she didn't see.

There were no tears.

"If I cry I'll fill the ocean," she said. "I won't be able to stop. It's better not to start. It's too late to start now, anyway."

Reflection

These are vignettes of a woman who has traversed the uncharted swamps of grief with grace and determination, realizing there was no finish line for anything she was going through, yet knowing she had to keep going for her family.

She told her story after all these years because it was one of the things, like eating salt fish, she thought might ease that tender spot that lies uneasily on her soul. I wrote it to recognize her loss. This book is me putting my hands on my mother's cheeks, looking her in the eye, and saying, "Catherine, you lost five children."

My greatest hope is that it acknowledges the unfathomableness of what she's endured. I want it to bring her a peace she's been searching for, likely without realizing it, for most of her life. I don't mean the kind of peace that comes with resolution but one that comes with understanding that she did the best she could with what she was faced with.

Knowing that it comes with a price of forgiveness for living, and perhaps making a stab at filling the ocean with tears, is a consequence I've no right to ask nor impose. But she will decide that for herself.

This book is also a tribute to my mother's resilience and strength at a time when both meant she didn't cry, and she pushed forward despite the pull to go back. It is a testament to how somebody can hold an unbelievable grief, to be alive without feeling alive, to breathe because it happens, and to remain upright and courageous in the face of the insurmountable because she wanted to protect the ones who remain.

My mother has lived a life of selflessness and kindness to others while managing the weight of emptiness and a suffocating absence that ceaselessly seeks notice. She has climbed mountains of grief and walked softly in its valleys as it shadows her to the end of her days. In her words, them that's gone through it are them that knows.

If my mother's story brings peace, charity of spirit toward those who need it, or gives strength to those who may feel hopeless or lost, she will know the worth of the courage it took to lay bare her life.

In gratefulness and love for the woman who raised me, I am blessed to have been influenced by such an amazing soul. She let what mattered in around her loss and never faltered in that. I was fortunate and am grateful to be one of the things that mattered.

I hope her story inspires you in even a small way to mend what may be less than whole in your life. If it is a loss that you are grieving and you come to understand you are never alone in that raw and wounded space, she will be comforted by that.

If her story gives you a fresh prospective on what is weighing heavy on your heart, and you find the courage to acknowledge it, face it, step through it or step with it, and move forward because she did it, then it has served a greater purpose. But in the end, I leave that with you to decide for yourself.

Glossary of Presence

The following are snippets of what our mother, mother-in-law, and grandmother externalized. Despite all she went through, she didn't allow it to interfere with her love and care for us.

Eddy

My earliest and fondest memory is of Mom and Dad taking me bakeapple picking. I was only seven or eight years old. Before going, she went to the store and bought a package of Milk Lunch biscuits to have on the marsh. When we got to Cape Dog River, Dad carried each of us across on his back, and I remembered feeling so safe, and I was certain Mom felt that way, too.

After picking berries, Dad made a fire and boiled water. Mom brewed tea in a can and shared around the biscuits. It was the nicest thing I'd ever tasted back then. We'd never had them before, so it was a real treat. It was one of the best days in my early memories. I've never had a Milk Lunch biscuit that I didn't think of that time.

We made many trips to the bogs and marshes after that, year after year, with more and more of us as the family got older. Mom made sure we had something nice for a lunch when we got there.

When we all got older and went out working, we wanted to give her things to make life easier on her. We knew she'd sacrificed a lot for us growing up. After Dad died, I liked to carry on that tradition. I'd ask Mom to come to Ontario for one of Anna or Patrick's church sacraments. She'd balk at times but usually said yes, and I'd send her a ticket.

She came up a few times in Lent, and we'd go to the Stations of the Cross at the church on Fridays. She enjoyed that. I'd ask if she wanted to stay for the Mass, and she'd say, "No, that's enough of that today." She knew I'd worked all week and didn't want to put me out. We'd all go as a family to Sunday Mass. It was nice to have her here and do those things with us.

One spring, I asked her to go to Mexico with our family. Mom fit right in, though she'd never been on a resort before. She sat around the pool. I thought she'd be stir-crazy, but that didn't happen. She enjoyed her time there.

Once, after Patrick had just gotten out of the pool and Irena had dried him off, he walked behind Mom's lounger chair at the same time that she got up. The chair moved, and she twisted and sent Patrick flying back into the pool. Once we got him out, we all laughed about it. Though Patrick doesn't remember it, it still brings a smile to my face.

While we were there, Mom called Marg to tell her where she was. Marg couldn't really hear her and asked, "Who's this?"

So, Mom says, "It's me, girl, I'm not gone that long that you don't know me." I could hear Marg laughing on the other end.

Mom was straightforward and real. She was fun to have around. We, especially the kids, loved her being with us, hated to see her go, and looked forward to when she'd return.

⁂

Irena

I looked forward to Mother's trips to our house. As soon as she'd arrive from the airport and see me on the step, she'd say, "For the love of God, come over here and give me a hug."

She wouldn't go home without making a fruitcake or boiled raisin cake for Ed. She'd send one in a parcel at Christmastime, too. We'd love to get her packages, because they were full of little things as well as gifts. It could be Santa pencils, or little ornaments, or chocolate snowmen, or who knows what. That was the fun of it. The children loved it.

Mother also baked Newfoundland tea buns when she was here. She complimented me on my pork roasts and looked for Polish sausages because she said I knew where to get the nice ones. Mother loved soups, too, and liked the Polish ones. She'd want me to make them all the time. She taught me how to make Jiggs' dinner, which my family and friends still enjoy.

When Mother stopped coming, I phoned her one day because I wanted to make the tea buns. She gave me the recipe. I took out all the ingredients and started. They smelled so nice, but when I opened the oven, I knew something was wrong.

I phoned Mother and told her the buns didn't grow. She started to laugh. She'd forgotten to tell me to add baking powder. She kept at me to try making them again, and when I did, they turned out so nice. Now when I make them, I think of Mother. She also tried to get me to bake bread, but I couldn't master using the yeast.

I love to see Mother and to hear her voice on the phone. She is kind and welcoming and never afraid to try new foods or go to new places. We miss her visits and her call to "Come over here and give me a hug."

Patrick

When Nanny came to stay with us, she'd take me for a walk every day to the doughnut shop and buy me a treat. She tried to get me to say "doughnut" because I used to call them "do-nuts." It wasn't to make fun but to hear me say it. If it was wet, she'd wait until somebody was around with a car and get them to take us both. Even when I got older, she'd get Dad or Mom to go to the doughnut shop and bring some back to the house.

Any time she was up, we'd get to go to extra baseball games at the SkyDome. Nanny loved baseball and was eager to go with us. She'd cheer, and I was surprised that she knew every player on the team and whether they were doing good or not.

Nanny liked hockey and knew I liked it, too. When I was younger, she would help me get on my goalie equipment and then spend hours out in the driveway taking shots at me. She was good, too, and it was hard to keep the goals out of the net. I enjoyed that time together.

When I got into video games, Nanny would make sure I'd have the newest one I wanted before she'd leave to go home. I miss Nanny's visits and can't pass the Country Corner store without thinking of her and smiling.

Anna

My earliest memories of Nanny are from when I was in elementary school. When I'd get home, if Nanny was here, I'd be confident that when I went to the fridge there would be a Boston cream doughnut sitting on the shelf. Every day it was there, and she knew it was my favourite.

At Christmastime she'd send gifts, and the ones I'd treasure the most were the things she made. She knitted me a fuzzy scarf one year, and I still wear it because I know it was her hands that put it together just for me.

When she was here and we'd be having supper, after everyone was finished, I'd ask Nanny if she wanted more. She would never fail to say, "No, I've had enough. I'm stuffed." But as soon as we had the dishes washed and put away, she'd be in the fridge. "Anna, I believe I'll have some more of that whatever you call it. It was some good." Then the two of us would laugh. I'd help her get whatever she wanted, and she'd be so happy. I loved to see her happy.

The most precious gift she ever gave me besides her love was a set of golden rosary beads belonging to her sister, May. One winter when Nanny was here, I'd often see her with the beads in her hands, and she'd be praying. She'd take them to the church with her when she went. I could see they meant a lot to her, and she always carried them. They'd be in her coat pocket or in her hands.

When we were driving her to the airport, Nanny and I were in the back seat of my dad's vehicle. She took the beads from her pocket and reached for my hand. When I opened my palm, she laid the beads there and then covered them with her warm hand.

"These are for you," she said. "They are to protect you. I know you are going through a hard time, and I've been praying for you."

I started to cry, and Nanny started to cry, and we hugged each other. Then she squeezed my hand over the beads again and nodded. "Remember, you are in my prayers." I never forgot that. Nanny was giving her love and healing to me the best way she knew how.

Neil

In North Harbour, when the kids were young, every Saturday or Sunday I liked to take everyone for a drive. Dad would get in the front with me and Trudy, and Mom would get in the back seat behind me and with the kids.

We wouldn't have left the yard when I'd feel a nudge on my arm. Mom would be pushing a folded $20 bill between the seat and the door and out of sight of everyone. It was no good refusing, because she'd make me take it. Then, wherever we went, if there was a store around, she'd ask me to stop. Mom took the kids in to get them something, and then she brought back drinks and chips or an ice cream for everyone else.

She didn't have a lot, herself, and she'd say she wanted to pay her way despite knowing we were going, anyway.

Mom was also unafraid to tackle anything. We had an outdoor cat named Brandi. He came home one night with his tongue almost slashed in half. Over the coming weeks, Brandi wouldn't eat nor drink and grew weak. Part of his tongue became hard and leathery. I thought we'd have to get him put down, and Mom didn't want to hear tell of that. She said she'd fix his tongue if she had somebody to hold him. I said I'd do that, so I put on a pair of thick leather gloves and held Brandi. He didn't protest when Mom got the scissors and cut off the bad piece of his tongue. When I laid him down, he went straight to his dish and ate and drank. He perked up after that.

We went to Toronto a few years later, and Mom said it was a sin to take the cat because he'd be stuck inside. She wanted us to leave him home. When he got caught in several snares a year later, Mom did what she could to keep Brandi alive. He perished despite her efforts, and she made sure he was buried. She was as good to the cat as she could be, and she thought hard of him when he was gone.

Trudy

From the first time I met Mudder (Mother), she treated me like one of her own. When Neil and I got married, we lived in the same yard, and she was there whenever I needed her.

I remember when Kirsten was four months old, I had to go for surgery. She stayed with Shayne and Kirsten until I got home. For the next six weeks, she came over every morning and got the kids up and looked after them. She'd put Kirsten in my arms so I could hold her.

When I got my driver's licence, Mudder tagged along wherever I went. Sometimes we'd get into the biggest snarls, but she didn't mind. Like when I had to go to Placentia one day, I borrowed Thomas Dalton's truck, and off the two of us went.

On the way back, as soon as we turned onto the pavement, I heard the pop, and the truck pulled to the side. I got out, and sure enough, we had a flat tire. Mudder got out, too, and the skies opened up and it poured on us. We got saturated.

An older man stopped and said he'd get Larry to come help us. We managed to get the tire off and the other one on before Larry arrived. He tightened the lug nuts for us and left, figuring we wouldn't be far behind.

Mudder got back in the truck and shut the door, but the door wouldn't close. She banged it two or three times, and no luck. I got out again and went around to her side and tried in vain to make the latch close.

"Get in, girl. I'll hold the door until we get to Thomas's place."

"Mudder, it's bad enough to go back after getting a flat, but I can't go back with a flat and the door not closing."

"Get in until the rain holds off," she said. I was drenched to the skin by now, so I jumped back in to get warm. When I closed the door, there was nothing but a bang. My door wouldn't close now, either.

We looked at each other, and she fell in across the seat laughing. "I can't believe the tangles I get into," she said as she shook with laughter, and so did I. I fiddled with the two doors until they finally closed. As soon as I put the truck in drive, the rain stopped. That sent the two of us into gales of laughter. We were like two drowned rats when we got to Thomas's place. All he did was laugh at us.

When Mudder came to Thompson to stay with us, we got a kitten named Simba. The kitten would get up on her lap or her puzzle book and go to sleep. We'd often come home from work, and Mudder would say she didn't want to stir because she'd wake the cat. It wasn't an imposition; she was quite content with the kitten asleep on her.

She loved all the dogs and cats we had over the years. If she stayed for a day or a week or a month, it was no trouble to find the pets. They'd be stretched out across her and asleep.

Mudder was only supposed to be with us in Thompson for a few weeks but didn't want us to be by ourselves at Christmas. So, she stayed well into the New Year. Before going home, she made seventy fish cakes for us and froze them because she knew we loved them.

Going home, we drove to Winnipeg, where she had her first experience staying in a hotel. Neil and I took her to watch curling before she flew out the next day. She decided to drop into Eddy's on the way and was gone, all told, nine months before she landed back in St. John's.

Kirsten

When I was a little girl, Nan babysat Shayne and me on the nights that Mom and Dad went to darts. Before bed, we'd ask Nan to get us cereal and milk. She'd no sooner have gotten it for us when we'd start laughing and carrying on. Nan would say, "Knock off that tittering," and that would send us over the edge. We'd laugh louder, and without meaning to, we'd spit milk everywhere. She'd tell us to knock it off again. It was just funny, and we couldn't help ourselves. The next week, it was the same thing. She never told on us, though. She'd say, "They were no trouble at all."

Any time she was watching me at her house, I'd stay up late and watch the hockey or baseball game with her and Pop. I remember I'd fight so hard to stay awake, but so often I'd fall asleep on the couch and wake up in a bed in the morning thanks to Nan.

Growing up with her next door, we could count on Nan to get us whatever we wanted to eat. I could go in and ask for anything from toast and tea to toutons. She'd whip up touton dough from scratch without a thought. This was nothing extraordinary in my mind back then; it's just what she did. She was a constant. Now I know how much work that would have been, but then, I think if I said I wanted the moon, I'd have it.

Everything that went on in the school, Nan would be there. She was like the community nan, because that's what all my friends called her, too. If I was playing basketball or having a piano recital, Nan was there. If we went for a drive, Nan was there. When I'd get sleepy, she'd tell me to come in under her wing. I'd wake up resting under her arm. She was an extension of Mom and Dad, and I just accepted and probably unknowingly expected her everywhere.

At Christmas, my favourite gift was Nan's wool socks, and now it's the same for my kids. They love visiting her and giving her hugs. She is supportive and loves us through words and actions, actions being the best part.

Shayne

I lived with Nan, and before that, I lived to Nan's. Growing up in the same meadow, I spent many hours with Nan and Pop. They were part of my everyday life, and I couldn't imagine living any other way. My first stop when I got off the bus was to go to Nan's before I went home. Sometimes, well, most times, Nan would be cooking something that I liked, and she'd have enough for me. Then, after eating with my grandparents, I'd go home to eat my supper. Nan warned me not to say I'd eaten there and that I'd better eat my supper at home so Mom wouldn't get mad with me.

After Pop died, I wouldn't let Nan stay by herself, so I moved in. If she was in North Harbour, I'd stay with her. It was as much my home as the one I had next door. It wasn't a decision; it was just a thing I did, same as breathing.

One of the nicest memories I have of Nan is the time I took her, Marg and Dick, and a few others to Maggoty Cove to go trouting. We had a boil-up out there and had a few casts of the line in the water. We didn't catch either trout, but listening to the conversations around the fire was priceless. Nan loved the outdoors, and I was happy that I could bring her that experience.

After she moved out to Mary's, when I came back from Alberta every few weeks, I'd pick her up to go home with me. One time, she said she wanted some cod nuggets from the grocery store to cook that night. On the way to the store, we were having a chat about when Nan and Pop raised chickens. Inside, she couldn't find what she wanted so she asked one of the workers if he could show her where the hens' nuggets were. When she realized what she said, she burst out laughing, then so did I. We were the longest time telling the man what we were looking for. He was not impressed.

That's the way it was with Nan. You never knew what you were getting into nor what the conversations would be. But I do know that she has the best sense of humour and is a pleasure to be around. I couldn't think how anyone would have it any better than I did growing up under the umbrella of love in that meadow.

Mary

When Mom lived with me, I used to take her somewhere on the weekends. She was always game to go. She'd say as long as the car was going ahead, she'd be in it. She never cared how long the drive was or the destination; she wanted to go.

A few times, we went down around the Burin Peninsula and stayed for a night or two. She was going for eighty years old when she wanted to walk to the site of the *Truxton* and *Pollux*. There was no stopping her, and she hiked that trail without issue. It was hard to keep up with her at times.

When I was turning sixty, Mom helped plan a surprise party for me. She got Ida to find friends of mine. She got me out of the house, made all kinds of food, and a big crowd showed up. I never knew a thing about it until I got home to a houseful. She was thoughtful and kind like that. If there was anything special, she'd make sure it was marked.

Scott

Of all the memories of my nan, I think the ones that stand out the most were when she lived with us. I used to help her learn the bus routes, and Nan caught on real fast. One day, it was snowing out, and a girl got on the bus with a tank top on. Nan looked at me and said, "I think she's going to get snow in her navel." The two of us laughed until we got home.

In the evenings, we often played games of cards like Queens and Auction. Nan could be at anything or talking to anyone and would drop it or say she had to go so she could play. She loved cards and was quick at them, too. You wouldn't get anything past her.

Every year that Mom went to her Christmas party at work, me and Nan would get in the spirit of things. We'd put up the tree and hang the decorations, place the candles in the window, and have everything festive so that it would be there when Mom got up in the morning.

When we were little and Nan and Pop lived in North Harbour, I was in the shed with one of my cousins when Pop's foot went through the floor. His head came down and smacked off the trailer, and he started to bleed. Now, I wasn't very fast, but that day, I outran everyone into the house, screaming for Nan because I knew she'd make it better. We all tore up over the stairs and told her Pop was bleeding. Nan made it to the shed before us, and got Pop out of the hole, and then she fixed him up. Nan made things better.

When my father died, Nan was staying with her sister that winter. But when I got back to the house, she was there waiting. She hugged me, and we cried together. I didn't see Nan cry until that day. I knew it was because I was crying, and I felt how much she loved me.

Nan has lots of love to give, and I feel lucky to be one of her grandchildren. Now that I have children of my own, she spreads that love to them. She made sure that she put a coin in

Cora's hand when she was born, wanting to give Cora her first money. That was important to her. Sadly, with the pandemic, she didn't get to do that for Abraham. But when they visit, Nan is so kind. She can't believe how big Abraham has gotten. He even high-fived her on the last visit. Though she doesn't see them often, I know how much she loves them. Nan is one of a kind.

Ida

New Years Eve, 2018, Mom and I were playing cards while waiting for the clock to pass into 2019. Thomas was working overnight and called to wish us a happy new year at midnight, so we stopped playing for a few minutes. NTV was showing fireworks while community names were scrolling across the screen. I was paying attention to the names waiting to tell Mom when North Harbour came up at the same time I hung up the phone. I happened to be glancing back and forth at the television when I picked up the cards.

"Whose turn is it?" Mom asked.

"It's yours," I said as I glanced once again at the names.

"The Jewers?" Mom said. "Are they any good?"

I looked at her under my brows. "Mom, girl, it's your turn," I said a little louder.

"George Burns," she said. "I thought he was dead."

I burst out laughing and repeated, "For the love of God, Mudder, it's your turn."

She started to shake with laughter. "Something getting wrong with me," she said as she reached for the deck of cards. We laughed about that for the next week.

Mom was game to help at whatever. If there was a crowd coming for dinner or supper, she'd be peeling vegetables or doing something. One time, we were having a fundraiser for one of the girls, who was going on a trip for soccer. Mom made over 200 toutons for me, which I sold packaged with a bowl of pea soup. She did that a second time the next week, again without question. She never cared how much work she had to do herself if it helped somebody. She'd never pass a place that a kid was selling tickets without buying some. She didn't care what the prize was; that didn't matter to her.

We had a few surprise birthday parties for her over the years. One time, it was on Woody Island, where she also became a model on their pamphlets and Internet site. Another time, we had a party for her at the community hall in North Harbour, and yet another at our house, where more than eighty people gathered so that they could surprise her. It struck me that Mom was humbled that anyone would do that for her when she would easily do it for others. That's who she is.

Thomas

Catherine was kind to me, to us, and to the girls. One of the things that I won't forget happened when we moved into our house in St. Bride's. We had nothing. I'm sure she thought to herself that we must be off our heads to have gotten married with nothing, no jobs, no future, just the crazy idea that we were doing the right thing. But she didn't say a thing.

She called us before we moved into the house we had under construction and asked us to come to North Harbour. That wasn't unusual, as we'd usually made a trip once a week. We had an old truck at the time and feared nothing like breaking down or bad tires. This day, she asked us to take her to Kelligrews in Conception Bay South and, coincidentally, not far from where we live now.

There was a second-hand furniture repair place that sold fridges and stoves. She knew we didn't have a fridge, so she bought us a gold-coloured one. It cost $250, which was a lot for us at the time and I'm sure a lot for her. But despite our protests, we went home with that fridge. We had it for about ten years before it gave out. I'll never forget her doing that for us and so many other things later. She didn't want us to speak of it nor pay her back. It was a gift, she said. She gave us a hand up when we needed it.

When she came to live with us, I finally had somebody around who would eat moose, fresh and salt fish, and fish cakes. I loved to cook salt fish for her, especially when she wasn't feeling the greatest. She said it boosted her up, and I liked that. But she worried that she was leaving me short. She'd often send me for a bucket of chicken. "Make sure you get enough for everyone," she'd say. She was kind and thought about the needs of others before herself.

Sharon

When we were really young, Nan would take us berry picking up on the hill behind her house. We'd eat or throw as many at each other as we picked. She didn't care. Then she'd make blueberry pies and muffins from scratch. It was always warm there, and we'd love to visit on the weekends. It wasn't only to hang out with our cousins, but seeing Nan and Pop was a real treat.

When we were in our teens, Nan went to our softball games. She'd sit on the bleachers for two or three hours and cheer us on. Looking back at it, I'm sure it was like watching paint dry, but she made it seem exciting. We'd be so proud to have fans in the stand when lots of others had nobody. All my friends called her Nan. She liked that. They'd hug her whenever they saw her. She was just nice to everyone. She'd make toutons for us after school, always bake bread, and offer toast whenever we wanted it. Nan's toast was the best.

One night, I got into beer with some of my friends, and we were all too young to be at it. Nan was babysitting and drove me to bed when I got home. She kept checking on me and found me asleep on my back at some point and made me turn over. "Get off your back or I'll tell your mother," she said. I was terrified that she'd tell and I'd get in trouble. But she never ratted me out, nor did she ever bring it up again after the next morning, when she told me not to do it again.

Nan was up for anything. We went to Gros Morne National Park, and she came along and slept in the tent with all of us. She'd climbed it the year before so didn't go with us that day, but she stayed at the campsite with us for a few days.

I always felt special with Nan, she had my back, and we'd laugh about the foolishest of things. What is the most special is that I have her name, Catherine, as my second name.

Stacey

When I think of Nan, there was the North Harbour Nan, the Mary's Nan, and the Our House Nan. No matter where she lived, she was just funny and loving, and it was nice to be around her.

In North Harbour, when we'd be driving through, we'd look for the blue butt on the hill where she'd be stooped picking berries. Just because the first time we saw her there, she was wearing blue capris, and she laughed when we told her about her blue butt. The North Harbour Nan had homemade toast, the good cheese spread, the best goulash ever, and it was warm and welcoming there.

The Mary's Nan was one we'd meet in the mall all the time. I knew if I was going to St. John's I'd go see Nan at the mall. We'd sit and talk. She'd have a $5 bill she'd want to give me whether I protested or not.

The Our House Nan was somebody who was there all the time, and that was nice. We'd all go to Tim Hortons together, or anywhere, really. The TV flickered in her room all night, and we'd see it through the crack in the door. She'd be asleep, but it didn't matter. It felt like she was just *there*.

One time, we were leaving the driveway and had just backed out on the road when Nan screamed and tried to pull open the car door. Mom stopped, and Nan jumped out. She started brushing herself off. We put down the window, and Nan was pure dancing on the side of the road.

"What's wrong, Nan?" all of us girls in the back asked.

"There's a flying ant on me," she said as she brushed herself off.

When she got back in the car a few moments later, I was concerned and asked, "Nan, are they dangerous?"

"Dangerous, they'd eat ya, that's how dangerous they are."

We all erupted into laughter, including Nan, now that she was safe from being eaten. She was just funny. I could laugh with her.

You knew that there was a youngster in the house because you'd hear Nan's, "toudle dee, loudle dee, loudle dee, louw," and sure enough, there'd be somebody's child bouncing on her knee and she'd have the biggest smile on her face.

Nan and I have this special thing where we touch our foreheads gently together. It's like this weird special thing where we connect for a few seconds, lock eyes, and we know we're doing it. Like a hug without the hug. Of course, we'd hug, too—but the head touch is just different. I can't visit Nan without doing that before I leave.

Nan is forever "tortured" thinking about everyone else's well-being despite anything she might have going on herself. She constantly has someone or something on her mind to pray over. If you had a job interview or were sick, even with a common cold or something, she would be "tortured" over that until you were better or she heard the results. And if you had good news to tell her, she'd usually cry with overwhelming happiness because she "tortured" herself (for no real reason, though it was real to her) thinking about your well-being.

Shawna

When the kids were born, Nan wanted to be the person that gave them their first money. She'd put a loonie in their hand as soon as she saw them for the first time. It was like a ritual and something she needed to do.

All my friends loved Nan. She was on many of their lists as somebody to visit at Christmastime. She'd have little stockings or treats for my friends' children, and she made sure there was a special bag for them at Halloween. She'd get her picture taken with the littlest ones on her knee.

When we were young, any time we saw Nan, she'd have a dollar for us, and later it would be five. She'd come to the house on the long weekend in May to make sure we had enough to get a pass for Thomas Amusements. We used to go on Friday night because we knew Nan would be there on Saturday and we'd get to go again.

One time, we were in North Harbour and the lights had gone in the house. A man from NL Power came up to the door. Nan warned me not to say anything to him. When she opened the door, I stood beside her. The man said something to Nan, and I looked at him.

"Mister, you got nar (neither) tooth in your head," I said, looking up at him as innocent as you please.

"Shut up, girl," Nan said, quickly. "You got neither one, either." And I didn't. All my front teeth on top and bottom were gone.

We still chuckle at that, and Nan has told it often.

One time when Nan was living with us, I got off the bus and had one of my friends with me. When I came in through the door, I could smell bread baking. When I got farther in, I saw Nan by the table with a pair of my underwear on her head. She used my underwear because she didn't have a hairnet. I was so embarrassed. But my friend didn't say anything. I guessed all nans did the same thing.

When Nan was living with Mary, she'd go to the Avalon Mall. If we wanted to see her, we'd look for the white head in the food court. There would be Nan. We'd get a cup of coffee for her and something for ourselves and sit down and have a chat. All my memories of Nan are good ones and make me smile.

Larry

When we were young, we were expected to help around the house, and most of the time we liked to do that. Once, when it was sheep-shearing time and Dad wasn't home, some of us boys rigged up a ladder across the rails on the little footbridge leading to the backyard. We'd catch the sheep in the back meadow and tie them on the ladder. We hoped that would make it easier for Mom.

By the time we got to the seventh or eight one, we weren't enjoying the sheep chasing as much, and it was getting a lot like work. They were hard to catch. So, we also weren't getting as good at tying them on. The last one we got up on the make-shift table was kicking a lot by the time Mom got ready to shear it. She was coming toward the sheep when it started kicking. I'm sure Mom must have been tired by then, too, because she held its head down and said, "I'll shove the scissors behind your ear and kill you if you kicks me."

We thought she meant it but didn't think she meant while maybe meaning it. We tied it down better, and the sheep lived, less its wool. We were more careful with the next ones, as we didn't want to be responsible for the welfare of the animal.

Mom was funny, though, and we never knew what she'd say. That's something I love the most about Mom, her sense of humour.

Caroline

We were in North Harbour one time for a visit just after Larry and I were married. There was a party in the hall, and we both went. When the party was over, we came back to the house. Neil invited us in, but I wanted to go visit with Catherine. The lights were all on, so I figured she was up.

Larry brought me to the back door, and I went in and up the stairs. Everything was quiet. I began to creep so I wouldn't wake anyone. I was halfway up the stairs when I heard a bear growl. I'd been camping for many years with the Girl Guides and was certain there was a bear in the house. Then it got quiet again, so I thought I'd been mistaken. I didn't know if there were bears in Newfoundland.

I took two more steps, and the bear growled again. I crouched on the stairs, not knowing if I should run or play dead. Things got quiet once more, so I thought maybe I'd had too much to drink and I was imagining it. I crept up the last of the steps, and the ungodly snarling growl came again. My eyes centred on where it was coming from, and it was Catherine snoring in the chair.

She woke with a start when I laughed. I told her what I thought was happening, and we both howled in laughter. She told everyone that I thought she was a bear. What a beautiful person to accept such grand and outlandish notions from a mainlander like myself.